The Bible Speaks Today

Series Editors: J. A. Motyer (OT)
John R. W. Stott (NT)

Songs from a Strange Land,
The Message of Psalms 42-51, John Goldingay

A Time to Mourn, and a Time to Dance,
The Message of Ecclesiastes, Derek Kidner

The Lord Is King,
The Message of Daniel, Ronald S. Wallace

The Day of the Lion,
The Message of Amos, J. A. Motyer

Christian Counter-Culture,
The Message of the Sermon on the Mount, John R. W. Stott

Guard the Gospel,
The Message of 2 Timothy, John R. W. Stott

I Saw Heaven Opened,
The Message of Revelation, Michael Wilcock

THE LORD IS KING

The Message of Daniel

Ronald S. Wallace

InterVarsity Press
Downers Grove
Illinois 60515

© Ronald S. Wallace
First American printing, June 1979, by
InterVarsity Press, with permission from
Universities and Colleges Christian Fellowship,
Leicester, England.

InterVarsity Press is the book-publishing division
of Inter-Varsity Christian Fellowship,
a student movement active on campus at hundreds
of universities, colleges and schools of
nursing. For information about local and regional
activities, write IVCF, 233 Langdon St., Madison, WI 53703.

Distributed in Canada through Inter-Varsity
Press, Canada, Unit 10, 1875 Leslie Street,
Toronto, Ontario M3B 2M5, Canada.

Unless otherwise stated, the Bible text in this
publication is from the Revised Standard
Version, copyrighted 1946, second edition 1971,
by the Division of Christian Education,
National Council of the Churches of Christ in
the United States of America, and used
by permission.

ISBN 0-87784-734-7
Library of Congress
Catalog Card Number: 79-1996

Printed in the United States of America

General preface

The Bible speaks today describes a series of both Old Testament and New Testament expositions, which are characterized by a threefold ideal: to expound the biblical text with accuracy, to relate it to contemporary life, and to be readable.

These books are, therefore, not 'commentaries', for the commentary seeks rather to elucidate the text than to apply it, and tends to be a work rather of reference than of literature. Nor, on the other hand, do they contain the kind of 'sermons' which attempt to be contemporary and readable, without taking Scripture seriously enough.

The contributors to this series will all be united in their conviction that God still speaks through what he has spoken, and that nothing is more necessary for the life, growth and health of churches or of Christians than that they should hear and heed what the Spirit is saying to them through his ancient—yet ever modern—Word.

J. A. MOTYER
J. R. W. STOTT
Series Editors

To
Shona
Kirsty Ann
Stewart
Murray
and Craig

Contents

Author's preface

EARLY in my ministry, when I had to spend much of my energy in preparing two Sunday sermons, I sometimes used the book of Daniel in Bible classes and at mid-week prayer meetings. Since I was otherwise so busy, I taught from it simply what came to me as a pastor as I read through the text in the available translations and thought about our situation in life as a group of ordinary people struggling somehow to know and do God's will in our day. Later on I was able to use better the commentaries I then had available at the manse, and I preached through the book chapter by chapter at our evening services. At a still later stage, when I became a teacher in a seminary, I also went through the book several times in courses of evening lectures prepared primarily for first-year students and lay people. Of course, by now I had the resources of a good library at hand, and I consulted everything available as introduction, background material and commentary.

It was at this last stage that I really had to face acutely for the first time the academic and pastoral problems of interpreting such a book for today. Daniel had by this time become an old and trusted friend to me, though, of course, he was not the type who made himself too readily familiar. He had always had a good deal to teach me and my people about God, Christ and prayer, the future of history and the way to live the Christian life. He had impressed himself on me no less than had men like Abraham and Moses and Elijah. I had believed he had been a leader of the people of God in exile. But now in the library I had been told through a whole corpus of modern exegesis that the book I had liked so much was not really about the exile at all, and that Daniel was a decidedly second-rate figure. Not only had he never been in Babylon, but also he was not even a man. The idea of him had arisen (the implication went) somehow as a common factor, discerned by an editor, in a group of disconnected legends from various Middle East countries, and the resultant photofit picture was so obviously artificial that with even a little discernment I should never have been taken in as I had been.

I had now, of course, to ask myself whether or not I had been deceiving myself about Daniel and his book, and I went back to it prepared, if need be, to be penitent, to consult seriously the impressive stack of notes I had taken, and to seek to accommodate in a fresh exposition as much as I could of what I had read. I read the text of the book again and again. It was like going back to an old friend about whom I had been hearing strange stories, only to find that they did not fit at all.

What came out finally was the exposition given here in print. I have to admit that I found the book asserting itself more strongly than I had expected over against the main thrust of what I had read about it, and more decisively than had been the case with other passages of Holy Scripture with which I had gone through a similar experience. I deliberately had to lay aside a good deal of material whose ingenuity I had even admired. I found, too, that I simply could not isolate the book, as so many scholars seem to manage to do, from its place in a canon of Holy Scripture that moves towards the New Testament and finds its fulfilment in Jesus Christ. And as for Daniel, I again found him there in Babylon in flesh and blood, with hands and feet, and a real face, in a struggle quite like that of our church today, inspiring confidence and giving guidance. I discovered, too, that the truth rings out much more clearly when the pastor is concerned with pastoral as well as academic responsibility.

It is always justifiable to try to publish current expositions of Holy Scripture, and when the Inter-Varsity Press expressed an interest, I gladly let them read the first draft of the work. They have been most encouraging. I have received much help from Alec Motyer, sometimes in settling on better forms of expression, sometimes in suggesting what proved to be useful expansions. My daughter Heather also helped me no less effectively with the language and arrangement and the typing too. I am grateful to Columbia Theological Seminary for giving me the time and the sabbatical leave to write.

R. S. W.

Introduction[1]

The historical background

THE book of Daniel opens with Nebuchadnezzar on the throne in Babylon. The Babylonian dynasty had replaced the Assyrian as the dominant power in the eastern Mediterranean region during the last quarter of the seventh century BC, and was firmly established when Nebuchadnezzar defeated the Egyptians at Carchemish in 605 BC. In 604 he had succeeded his father on the throne. He still continued his father's conquests, and according to the account we have in the book of Kings, in 587–586 he finally subdued Judah and sacked Jerusalem, carrying a large section of the population back with him to Babylon. The book of Daniel assumes that there had been an earlier invasion of Judah in which he carried off some captives, including Daniel.[2]

After Nebuchadnezzar's death in 562 his sons and grandsons proved worthless, and in 556 a revolution ultimately placed on the throne an outsider called Nabonidus. His son was Belshazzar, who seems to have been ruling in Babylon as his father's deputy when the empire fell to the Persians under Cyrus in 539. After this the Near East was ruled for two centuries by a succession of Persian rulers. Of these, Darius the first was historically the best known. Then, late in the fourth century, came the dramatic overthrow of the Persian Empire by Alexander the Great who established Greek supremacy over the whole area in 331 BC. Some years after Alexander's death his Near East Kingdom was split in

---

[1]For a full discussion of problems related to the history, authorship, dating, *etc.*, of the book of Daniel, see J. G. Baldwin, *Daniel* (Tyndale Old Testament Commentary, Inter-Varsity Press, 1978). The introductory material here is limited to what directly serves the expository aims of the present series.

[2]*Cf.* 1:1, *i.e. c.* 605 BC.

two. The Ptolemaic dynasty, named after its first ruler Ptolemy I Soter, ruled the area around Egypt, and the Seleucid dynasty, named after its first ruler Seleucus I Nicator, tended to dominate Syria and Palestine. Between the two houses there was sometimes inter-marriage, sometimes plotting and treachery. The Egyptian Ptolemies were dominant till, in 198, the Seleucid Antiochus the Great defeated Ptolemy Epiphanes and finally obtained undisputed ascendancy over Palestine. The most important development, as far as the Jews were concerned, took place in 175, when after some intrigue Antiochus IV Epiphanes secured the Seleucid throne. To the person, career and ambitions of this one ruler a great deal of attention is given in the book of Daniel.

During this whole period the circumstances of the people of God changed greatly. As exiles in Babylon under Nebuchadnezzar they had to face the problems both of settling down in an alien land, dominated by a pagan religion, and also of remaining faithful to the God of their fathers, even though they had no temple and no sacrificial ritual. Daniel and his three companions are examples of how the faithful among them were able to do this triumphantly. After the accession of Cyrus the Persian in 539 some of the exiles returned to Palestine, and the numbers gradually increased till first the temple and then the walls were rebuilt. The Persian emperors were, on the whole, friendly and the returned community enjoyed a fair measure of religious liberty under their rule. But under the Greek empire they had to face a more severe threat than had come to any of them even in exile. Alexander the Great had had the ambition not only to conquer the world, but also to 'Hellenize' it, *i.e.* to bring everything under the influence of the Greek spirit. He set the process of Hellenization in motion and those who followed him succeeded to a remarkable extent.

Greek manners and ways of looking at everything spread. What was Greek seemed to saturate everything else with itself and to become universal. The influence of Greek culture permeated the ancient religions of the East and produced the Hellenistic mystery religions.

For many generations the Jewish nation as a whole succeeded in resisting this movement, for in Palestine under Ptolemaic rule no extraneous pressure was put on the population to conform to Greek ways. But within the Jewish community itself, especially amongst the 'intellectual' and priestly circles and amongst those

14

involved in the power politics of their day, there arose a strong Hellenizing party.

When Antiochus Epiphanes obtained power in Syria and Palestine he launched out on a determined and unscrupulous campaign of forcing Hellenism on the whole population, using enticement, bribery and intrigue, and ruthlessly destroying all open resistance. The story of his manoeuvres, his successes, and his ultimate failure can be read in the books of Maccabees. Even before his rule started the position of high priest at Jerusalem became vacant, and he was bribed to have Jason, one of the leaders of the Hellenizing party, appointed. This step was followed by the setting up of a school in Jerusalem where Jewish youths could be trained in Greek ways, to play Greek games and adopt Greek fashions. As the Hellenizing programme went forward there were deeper intrigues, and an unscrupulous impostor, Menelaus, supplanted Jason in the favour of the king. Under Menelaus as high priest more strife and intrigue followed, leading to massacre in the streets, the establishment of a Syrian garrison in the city, the flight of refugees and the issue of edicts forbidding the religious practice of the Jewish people. The punishment for infringement was death. Orders were given for the temple to be dedicated to the worship of Zeus Olympus and in the year 168 an altar to Zeus was erected in the temple and offerings were made on it. Heathen gods were to be honoured elsewhere; the eating of 'unclean' foods was compulsory. The edicts were brutally enforced. There were many massacres and many martyrs.

Determined resistance came from two parties. The Maccabean party under the inspiration and leadership of Mattathias, a country priest, and his sons, stirred up armed resistance, took to the field in battle and was ultimately successful. The other resistance party was called the Hasidim, or the 'holy ones'. They were a 'separatist' party whose policy was passive resistance and strict faithfulness to the law, especially at certain points which to them seemed to become crucial issues, such as the laws forbidding the eating of certain foods. Even during the fighting they did not offer resistance on the sabbath day and allowed themselves to be mercilessly cut down. These two parties came together for a time. At one point, for example, the Maccabees actually suspended the observance of the sabbath, thus encouraging the Hasidim to overcome one of their scruples. On the whole, however, the latter desired to remain independent of powerful political support, and to trust in God alone. There were deep differences in the ideas and outlook of each group.

This period, from 605 to 165 BC, is the span of history which the writer of Daniel is immediately concerned to speak about in any detail in the book. Other events may also be referred to in a more obscure and hidden way.

The traditional view of the book

The traditional view takes the book at its face value and affirms that it was written in Babylon by one Daniel who was himself a model of faithfulness, wisdom and piety for his times. Its purpose was to show how such a man and those around him triumphed by the grace of God during their exile; how the great tradition of their forefathers was kept alive by strict piety and discipline; and how persecution was overcome by faithfulness, courage and wisdom. Future hope was kept alive and sober by a series of prophetic visions given to Daniel. These outlined the difficult and changeable course through which world history would develop, and foretold especially the severe time of persecution the nation would come through under later foreign domination. They described, too, the tribulations and triumphs the people of God would share in as the days of the end of the world and the coming of the Messiah approached.

Among those scholars who hold such a general view of the origin and purpose of the book, there are great varieties of interpretation when it comes to many of the details. They differ, for example, when they attempt to define which succession of world empires is referred to in the descriptions of the various symbols of power: for instance, of the various metals, which make up the colossus in Nebuchadnezzar's dream in the second chapter, or of the various beasts, which succeed each other at the centre of world history in the seventh chapter. There is disagreement, moreover, on exactly which anti-God ruler was originally intended in the description of the little horn which displaced all the other horns of the fourth beast as it grew to such gigantic proportions and began to speak such sinister blasphemies (7:20f.). There is also marked difference of opinion on whether or not a description of the work of Christ was directly intended in the prophecy of what was to happen at the end of the 'seventy weeks' in Daniel 9:24, and on whether towards the end of the eleventh chapter there is a sudden transition of thought from the actual time of Antiochus Epiphanes into a distant messianic future (in 11:36).

The theory of the Maccabean orientation of the book

It is widely held today, however, that Daniel could not have been written in Babylon in the sixth century BC, and that it was never intended to be a faithful historical account of the time of the exile. The way in which the writer refers to the history of the Babylonian period is held, on this view, to be vague and unreliable. For example, it is alleged that the book begins with the erroneous supposition that there was an early siege of Jerusalem in the third year of the reign of Jehoiakim in 605 BC (1:1). It is pointed out that Belshazzar was not the son of Nebuchadnezzar, but of Nabonidus (5:11), and that he was never actually king of Babylonia as the story seems to imply. It is insisted that there is no evidence in history outside the book of Daniel for any 'Darius the Mede' who is said to have succeeded Belshazzar (5:31), nor of a Median empire in between that of Babylon and Persia, as the dreams and visions of the book seem to imply.

So much, then—so the argument goes—for the writer's knowledge of sixth-century Babylon! On the other hand, when it comes to describing the period of the Seleucid domination of Palestine, it is alleged that his references are much more detailed and very accurate, showing a specially intimate knowledge of the history leading up to the rise of Antiochus Epiphanes and of the details of his career and policy. Arguments along this line lead many scholars to the conclusion that the book originated not in Babylon but in Palestine and in Maccabean times.

In confirmation of this view other evidence is given. It is argued that if a man from Judah by the name of Daniel really occupied such a prominent position in the Babylonian Empire of the sixth century as is accorded to him in the book, then there would surely be some references to him in contemporary prophetic literature. Yet the only other references to anyone called Daniel in the whole of the old Testament literature are found in Ezekiel,[1] where the name Daniel seems to refer to a wise man who lived in the distant past and who had already become by long tradition classified in the Hebrew mind with men like Noah and Job. It is pointed out

[1]Ezk. 14:14, 20; 28:3.

that the earliest references to the book of Daniel itself are found only after the Maccabean period.

A study of the actual language used in the book is held to support the claim that it must have been written much later than the sixth century BC. The use of certain Greek words in the text seems to indicate a date after Alexander's conquest, and the use of certain Persian words in the text is regarded as having been impossible at the time of the Babylonian captivity. A whole central section of the book, moreover, is written not in Hebrew but Aramaic, and it is asserted that the form of Aramaic used in this section is similar to that used in Palestine in the second century BC. Why, it is asked, would an exile in Babylon in the sixth century have resorted to the use of such language? The Hebrew, too, it is asserted, is more like later than exilic Hebrew.

Further arguments in favour of the late dating of the book are derived from its position in the Jewish canon. In the Hebrew Massoretic editions the book is placed not among the 'prophets', but among the 'writings'. This is held to indicate that by the time the book of Daniel was current, the Hebrew prophetic canon was finalized. This view is strengthened by the argument that the book is a typical, though outstanding, example of the pseudonymous 'apocalyptic' type of literature that began to be produced in the second century BC and flourished for a lengthy period only after this date.[1] Moreover, it is argued that some of the theological views expressed in the book, especially the belief in a resurrection of the just and unjust from the dead, are late.

Those who believe that such evidence is decisive hold that the book of Daniel was issued originally as a tract, written probably by one of the Hasidim party to remind his persecuted contemporaries that Yahweh their God understood their plight, to assure them from these traditional stories that great men had triumphantly come through such things in past centuries by the grace of God, to set before them an ideal of faithfulness to the law and patient suffering, and to encourage them with visions of God's sovereign control, and of his future purpose of glory for his people. These truths and lessons remain intact, of course, on either of the main interpretations of the book, but in relation to the Maccabean date it is said that the writer desired to hide his identity and to conceal the message so that it would not be understood by the persecutors, but so that it could be read in its

[1]See below, pp. 24 ff.

hidden meaning by the circle it was intended to help. In answer to objections that our Lord himself seemed to believe that Daniel was the author of the book,[1] and that the theory tends to brand the book as a 'forgery', the reply is given that to attribute one's own writing to a great figure of earlier history was an accepted and respectable fashion in the days of apocalyptic writing, and that our Lord himself deliberately accepted certain limitations within the realm of his human knowledge with regard to such matters.

The answer from the conservative point of view[2]

Our reaction to such a theory of the book will depend to some extent on our belief about the nature of Holy Scripture. Many find it exceedingly difficult, for example, to see it as other than fraudulent (however 'pious' the motive) to try to pass off one's book under another and more influential name. Such a book, within Holy Scripture, appears to them to besmirch the holiness of God, just as factual or historical error seems incompatible with the God 'who never lies'.[3] Pressed along these lines, we are bound, for example, to marshal arguments in favour of the text at points where its veracity has been challenged. It is not really very difficult to defend the notion of a Babylonian invasion of Judah in 605 BC or the person of Darius the Mede. Indeed no proof has ever been brought forward that there was not, or could not have been, such an invasion or that there was not and could not have been any such person. Nor does the fact that the book of Daniel was not mentioned till the second century necessarily mean that it did not exist till then. Moreover we can argue that the author was merely speaking in a loose and customary way when he called Belshazzar the son of Nebuchadnezzar and did not really mean exactly this. 'Darius the Mede', too, could have been a fancy name for some temporary regent who took over Babylon for Cyrus. So the counter-arguments go on; and it is good that we should realize that they are pressed home with as impressive a display of scholarship as is used on the other side—especially when it comes to the discussion of the possible times when the Greek and Persian words could have been used. Some conservative scholars

---

[1] Mt. 24:15; Mk. 13:14.
[2] See further D. J. Wiseman and others, *Notes on some Problems in the Book of Daniel* (Inter-Varsity Press, 1965).
[3] Tit. 1:2.

seem willing to concede that some of the words in Aramaic used in the book could have been altered in later editions so that the later text as we now have it is different from the original one.

The central theme of the book—its convincing unity and integrity

Whatever decision we make about the origin of the book we must take into account that the consistent central theme of the book is different from that suggested by the theory that it is a tract for Maccabean times, and that the book has a unity and integrity that is not accounted for on this theory.

The theory, for instance, fails to deal adequately with the opening stories of the book or to take their thrust and message seriously. It places the whole centre of gravity in the later half of the work. The 'Babylonian' portion tends to become for some a mere introductory framework added after the book was written to help to provide the name of an anonymous author for the later visions. It is claimed that these stories had originally no close connection with each other. They were early stories which circulated originally in Babylonia and filtered through into Palestine about the time the Maccabean author was writing his work. He is said to have altered some of the stories to suit his purpose. There was, for example, a story about a mental illness which attacked Nabonidus for ten years and from which he was cured by a Jewish exorcist. This he is said to have taken and grafted on to the better-known Nebuchadnezzar to form the basis of the fourth chapter. Again, the Belshazzar story in the fifth chapter is sometimes regarded as a later and rather pointless insertion into the cycle.

The question, however, immediately arises: if the book is intended to be a tract with parallels being drawn between the days of the Babylonian captivity and the Maccabean persecution, why did the writer not try to make the Babylonian story fit better into the times he is supposed to have been writing for? Why did he not choose more relevant stories; and if he was going to change them, why did he not make a decent job of the whole thing?

The picture given in the book of Nebuchadnezzar is of one who became basically a benevolent God-fearing ruler, ready to listen to the word of God and to repent under it. It seems impossible to imagine that a tractist should invent such an inept parallel to the circumstances to which he was trying to address himself.

The point here at issue becomes simple and decisive: the theory of the Maccabean origin of the book fails to see the integral and subtle unity that runs through the whole book. When we begin at the beginning, study the opening chapters carefully, absorb their meaning, try to get their message, and from this start move on to the later chapters, we find that from start to finish the book has an extremely solid and satisfying unity. Proponents of the Maccabean theory find this unity awkward. Originally they divided the book into two distinct sections, making the last six chapters form the Maccabean nucleus and the first six a peripheral introduction. But attention was drawn to the fact that the seventh chapter of the book, like the previous five, is Aramaic and is obviously linked up in closest unity of thought to the second chapter. In response to this clear difficulty the division was altered to suggest that chapters 8 to 12 were the original tract. But examination will show that these later chapters are simply variations of the theme enunciated in the seventh chapter; they grow out of it, and look back to it. Moreover, the glimpses we have of Daniel in these later chapters are all subtly interwoven with the pictures of him in the first chapters.

When the unity of the book is recognized, then, the first chapters, which are themselves so vivid and profound in their thought, and so dynamic in their message, tend to dominate the exposition of the remainder of the book and thus to alter the entire approach to the later chapters.

Throughout the whole book it becomes obvious that the work is written as a message not primarily for those who are suffering in the midst of deadly persecution but rather for those who are living in a settled condition yet within an alien culture—in other words, not in a Maccabean-type situation, but in a Babylonian-type situation. In this situation what is required is the steady pursuit of the good life as far as the environment will allow it, faithful co-operation with those in authority as far as conscience will permit, strict adherence to the customs of the law in spite of the opposition that might occur, the cultivation of regular habits of devotion, a pride in the nation's religious traditions and a willingness to listen to others telling their visions and dreams, and taking an active part in political life and even accepting high office. Indeed, when we come to the so-called 'apocalyptic' chapters in the second section of the book we find the same message of steadfastness in going about the secular business of government, of the importance of regular prayer and Bible study. Their message is not one of how to live in the last days under severe tribulation, but one of how to live in settled times, maintaining a sober view of the future possible evil developments, and working so as to prevent if possible such developments. This does not seem to be the type of message or the type of book one would deliberately write for people who had to live through the days of Antiochus.

The book, therefore, may be assumed to have been there, current in some way, perhaps unappreciated even by those for whom it had been originally written—'sealed', so to speak[1]—yet a genuine word of God from the tradition of Israel's days in Babylon for all time to come for the people of God who might find themselves again a church in the wilderness, or in exile. In the situation which came upon the people of God in the days of Antiochus Epiphanes, the book written especially for the days of the exile was seen to have fresh possibilities of relevance, perhaps hitherto unsuspected, for the new situation of the people of God. Though originally addressed to different circumstances, it conveyed very powerfully at that later time of fearful persecution a message of encouragement, wise counsel, especially through its assurance that God had control and foreknowledge of the forces that seemed to dominate human history. There is no difficulty in holding that as it was issued afresh to apply itself to the circumstances of that day, it passed through a fresh version.

Daniel within the biblical tradition

In the order of Old Testament books as they appear in the Hebrew canon, Daniel is placed in the third division, the Writings, and not among the Prophets. In the Septuagint, however, it appears in the same place as in English versions of the Bible. This variation of place may indicate that it was found difficult to define the exact place of this book within the canon. It can hardly be claimed that Daniel writes like a prophet. While there are elements in his thought and ministry that could justify our classifying him as such, he embodies in his person more clearly the characteristics of the truly 'wise' man as these are described in the biblical tradition, and his writing and outlook are often now described as apocalyptic.

[1] *Cf.* 12:9.

We must therefore turn to explore the relationship of the book of Daniel to these three types of thought and literature.

a. Daniel within the prophetic tradition

There is some justification for placing Daniel among the prophets. He pored over their books. The chief concern of his life was that of all the prophets, and he lived and prayed for it as they did, that God's promises for his people as a nation might come to a true fulfilment in spite of their sins.[1] In his attitude towards the affairs of this world and his outlook on the future of this world he shared much of what was characteristic of the prophetic tradition. It is our purpose in the next section to describe the world-view and outlook on the future which is often called 'apocalyptic' in order to contrast it with the prophetic world-view and outlook on the future. It is our purpose here to underline certain of these characteristics of the prophetic view of the future that we believe helped also to make up that of Daniel.

When they describe what is to happen in the future, the prophets sometimes paint a picture quite different from that painted by later (Jewish) apocalyptics. As they look forward to what is to happen in the 'latter days' on this earth, they often give us ideal pictures of paradise being restored within the development and transformation of this earth's history itself, of a golden age arising out of the present age, either blending with it now or developing alongside of it.[2] They sometimes picture the Messiah who will rule in these days as an earthly prince and ideal ruler arising out of the house of David.[3] They urge their hearers to make this their goal, and indeed their achievement, as they wait upon God and, in true repentance,[4] seek his justice[5] and his presence in their midst,[6] believing that his Spirit is able to bring about this kind of fulfilment. In this way they will become a light to the nations.[7]

Daniel is obviously a man at home with this prophetic outlook and viewpoint. His long and intense prayer, inspired by the prophetic writings and especially by the reading of Jeremiah, shows his concern for the fulfilment of the Messianic and Davidic promises.[8] Sin, righteousness, mercy and forgiveness are his themes as they were those of the prophets. He shares their concern for social justice and for the relief of the oppressed, and when occasion allowed it he could preach just like a prophet.[9]

[1] Cf. 9:3 ff.   [2] Is. 2:1 ff.; 11:6-9; Am. 9:13 ff.   [3] Is. 11:1 ff.
[4] Ho. 14:1 ff.   [5] Am. 5:14 ff., 24.   [6] Is. 58.   [7] Is. 49:6 ff.
[8] Dn. 9:1-19.   [9] Dn. 4:27.

b. Daniel within the apocalyptic tradition

The book of Daniel is sometimes classed as an apocalyptic book. This indicates that it shares in the tradition of thought and style of writing given that name. By the second century BC it was clear that the living voice of prophecy which had inspired and dominated the religious and moral life in Israel for centuries had ceased completely. At this time there appeared instead a new series of writings, all with similar features in their form, technique and common outlook. These writings were popular and influential and were in the style now known and classified as apocalyptic. The authors believed the end of this age was approaching. In conveying and vindicating their message they claimed that the revelations they were issuing were originally given in the distant past to some well-known figure in history. There were, for example, the books of Enoch, and apocalypses attributed to Baruch, Moses and Abraham. It added authority to the message for the writer to hide his identity and to put his message as if it were a prophecy or dream given centuries before. Historical and contemporary events could thus be referred to as if they had been prophesied centuries before. Their revelations then described God's secret plan for the end of the ages with the use of terms and symbols similar to those used in the book of Daniel.

This apocalyptic thought and literature flourished especially during the period between the Testaments, but the apocalyptic outlook expressed in the great body of literature which was then produced had some of its roots in the teachings of the great prophets of Israel, as well as in the book of Daniel. Moreover, later, aspects of the teachings of these apocalyptic writings were adapted by Jesus in his teaching about the kingdom and the end of the world.[2] Thus a Christian apocalyptic tradition finds expression in the other parts of the New Testament,[3] and of course is given supreme expression in the book of Revelation. We can thus take note of the fact that there were elements in the developing apocalyptic outlook that found favour with Jesus himself.

The origin of much that is valid in this apocalyptic outlook (indeed those elements of it that found favour with Jesus) is to be found in the writings of the prophets of the Old Testament. We have already noted one distinct strand in the thinking of the prophets about the future, pointing out those passages in which

[1] *Cf.* Mk. 13.   [2] *E.g.* 2 Thes. 2:1–12.

they often express their hope of seeing the kingdom of God coming on this earth as a development and transformation of human history and a restoration of paradise lost.[1] There is, however, a second distinct strand of thinking about the future which twines itself round this latter strand and seems to develop with it, but which never seems to unite with it to provide us with one simple and satisfactory picture of how history will move finally to its climax, and how the kingdom of God will come. It is in this second way of thinking and writing about history and the age to come that we find the source of what is best in the apocalyptic literature.

In this apocalyptic view of the future the age to come is thought of only as succeeding a time of judgment in which the wicked and even the whole earth will be destroyed.[2] Sometimes even the great prophets have experiences of visions of another world above and beyond what is present on the earthly scene of history.[3] They seem to see God in this realm 'above', standing or sitting and directing his heavenly messengers.[4] Sometimes they too see visions so strange and difficult that heavenly beings are required to interpret these.[5] Sometimes too they give us vivid though vague pictures of an end-of-the-world history that is already being planned and set in motion from that other world, invoking cosmic disturbance embracing all nations; invoking too a tremendous conflict between good and alien forces that is to be undergone before the end of this age takes place and the new age is ushered in.[6]

The later extra-biblical apocalyptic writings which appeared towards the end of the second century BC took up such features in the prophetic writings and developed them in a way that did not always give a true expression of the thinking of the Hebrew prophets. In such later writings, a clear distinction is also drawn between the realm of earth and that of heaven. This present world is regarded as the sphere of an intense conflict between God and the sinister forces of evil. This conflict involves the heavenly realm as well as the earthly. The kingdom of God is regarded as wholly other than any earthly kingdom could ever become, and is expected to break in suddenly from beyond. The end of the old age will involve intense activity by the supernatural evil powers that

---

[1]See p. 23. [2]Is. 24:1 ff. [3]Is. 6:1 ff.
[4]E.g. 1 Ki. 22:19; Ezk. 1:1 ff.; 8:1 ff. [5]E.g. Zc. 1:8 ff.; 2:2 ff.
[6]E.g. Ezk. 38, 39; Zc. 12–14.

are already dominating it. As the new age breaks in there will be signs of cosmic disturbance in nature and great upheavals in history. The history of the earth will move in a series of dramatic and readily identifiable events according to a predetermined pattern and in recognizable periods. Everything that is old and evil will finally pass away in a cataclysmic happening that will shake all foundations and allow only what is of the will of God to survive.

The knowledge of these events and the key to their understanding can be communicated beforehand to initiated servants who are given insight into the mystery of God's purpose and his wisdom in what he is going to do. These revelations are communicated by visions, dreams and angelic messages whose truth and meaning are unfolded as time passes. Mysterious sacred numbers and strange animal symbols standing for various earthly agencies and powers are used.

The book of Daniel obviously had a central place in the formation of the apocalyptic tradition. Much of it was obviously cast into a literary form that became a model for the later writers. Daniel, himself, uses mysterious numbers[1] and symbols,[2] receives visions,[3] and forecasts history in detail in very much the same way as the authors of the standard works of Jewish apocalyptic literature.[4] There are other formal affinities between him and those who developed the late apocalyptic viewpoint. For instance, the backdrop of Daniel's visions is painted so as to emphasize very clearly the distinction between the two realms of heaven and earth,[5] and in his view of the future he sees the coming kingdom of God as contrasting very dramatically with the present kingdoms of this world.[6]

Yet it is to be noted that while Daniel helped so decisively to give shape to this important tradition, he nevertheless kept his thought strictly in accord with the word of God as it had then been expressed in the prophetic tradition, and he did not give way to the undesirable developments that took place within the apocalyptic literature of the later Judaistic period.

As we read this literature it becomes obvious where these later writers have gone astray. Their thought is often marked by a hopelessly deep cleavage between the present age and that to come. The present age is often regarded as so fully dominated by

[1]*E.g.* 9:24 ff.   [2]*E.g.* 8:3 ff.   [3]*E.g.* 10:5 ff.   [4]*E.g.* 11:2 ff.
[5]*E.g.* 7:9 ff.   [6]*E.g.* 7:12 ff.

evil that it has been given up to evil, only to run out its course to a finish when the kingdom of God will break in entirely from beyond. A very fatalistic view is often taken of how things are bound to work themselves out in the earth's history, and the worth of this world, its culture and possibilities are estimated from a very pessimistic viewpoint.

It is remarkable indeed that in the midst of all the formal similarities between his and the writings of these later authors, Daniel avoids any serious deviation from what is basic and central to the outlook on creation, providence and history held in the other writings of the biblical canon. He makes no concession to the pessimistic outlook on the world and the ultimately dualistic view of the relation between good and evil embodied in some of these 'apocalyptic' works. Moreover, he sees the kingdom of God powerfully at work within the present historical processes. His main affinity is always with the great prophets who were his predecessors and contemporaries.

c. Daniel and the wisdom tradition in Israel

When we read the first chapters of Daniel we cannot help noticing the parallels that can be drawn between Daniel at the court of Nebuchadnezzar and Joseph at the court of Pharaoh. Both men were exiles, showed exemplary alliegance to God and his law, underwent deep humiliation through being falsely accused, and were ultimately vindicated. Both obtained recognition for their gifts through their ability to interpret an important dream which had greatly troubled their king, and which no other magician had been able to unravel satisfactorily. Both became confidants of the king and were given second place only to him in the government of the realm. Both men were recognized as having extraordinary gifts from God, were classed as outstanding among those who were 'wise', and were associated with the other wise men of the court.

All over the Near East, wherever there was a centre of strong and prosperous government, there tended to develop a tradition of wisdom, sharing much in common with that of other capitals, yet preserving also local characteristics. This general wisdom tradition gave rise to a literature of its own in the form of proverbs, riddles, fables, stories and wise counsels. This literature took shape early in history. It was used in the schools of wisdom connected with court circles. The aim of these schools was to teach rules for success and happiness in life, and such practical worldly prudence in affairs as might help and guide kings and also train others for court positions of leadership and responsibility. The training included education in all the general branches of knowledge, the skills expected in those days of a scribe, and also such esoteric teaching as dream interpretation and astrology. It was mainly secular, for its religious associations did not affect it deeply.

Wisdom writings are known, both in Egypt and Mesopotamia, and in the Far East from 2500 BC onwards, and there is no reason to be sceptical about the very strong biblical tradition associating David, and especially Solomon, with this wisdom tradition. The literary products of Israelite wisdom are found in the books of Ecclesiastes, Job, Proverbs and the Song of Solomon, and wise men who gave counsel appear occasionally in such figures as Ahitophel and Hushai.[1] As it was absorbed into the life and literature of Israel, however, the general wisdom tradition from the surrounding nations was purged of its deep secularity and oriented at its centre to faith in God. This did not necessarily involve much alteration in its practical, commonsense content, and there are many parallels between the biblical book of Proverbs, for example, and those of Egyptian wisdom. But Israelite wisdom raised the ethical tone of the tradition and stressed the fact that for all the truest insights and the wisest practical guidance the inspiration of God's Spirit was necessary. In such figures as Joseph and Daniel we are shown how the wise man receives his inspiration and strength from above and is able to serve God and conduct his personal affairs and political duties far better than those who are merely trained on the world's schools of wisdom.[2] The best and most practical wisdom comes from above, and the fear of the Lord is its beginning.[3] This is the central aspect of the teaching of the Old Testament wisdom books. Daniel's prayer for enlightenment before he tries to interpret Nebuchadnezzar's dream is made up of texts taken from the wisdom literature of his own nation. He describes his experience of illumination in terms exactly parallel to those used there, and he shows better practical and political insight in the affairs of state than any of the other experts around him,[4] for this sphere as well as all the other aspects of life belongs to God. Daniel excels in

[1] 2 Sa. 16:23; 17:7, 14.   [2] Gn. 41:1 ff. Dn. 12:27 ff.   [3] Dn. 12:20 ff.
[4] 2:20.

28

prudence and tact which are also aspects of wisdom.[1] Moreover, he is the embodiment of a genuine deep piety in which every problem is related to God, the Word is searched for counsel and guidance, and the law itself is found to be a source of inspiration and communion with God.[2]

Note to the reader

This book is written with continuous reference to the actual text of the book of Daniel. The exposition will be best understood if the text of the relevant chapters of the Bible itself is read beforehand, kept open, and constantly referred to. The references to the the other chapters of Daniel, and to other parts of the Bible (often given at the foot of the page) should also be consulted.

[1] 1 : 8 ff.; 2 : 27 ff.; 6 : 3 ff.   [2] 6 : 10 ff.; 9 : 2 ff.

Daniel 1
The issue and the answer

The people of God: new questions in theology and policy

IN the third year of the reign of Jehoiakim king of Judah, Nebuchadnezzar king of Babylon came to Jerusalem and besieged it. And the Lord gave Jehoiakim king of Judah into his hand, with some of the vessels of the house of God (1:1, 2a).

When all this actually happened most of the people of Judah had to change their views about how God was going to work out his purpose for them within human history, and fulfil his promises. They had been led astray in their thinking and planning by an interpretation of the Word of God too much in accord with their own self-centred desires. Their scriptures, as they had read them, and their tradition, as they had interpreted it, had seemed to teach them that God's way of fulfilling his purposes for their nation was to be marked by certain unalterable principles. The royal line of David was to continue uninterrupted, and indeed undisturbed, till the glorious second David, the promised Messiah, his lineal successor, appeared on his throne in Judaea. Under his reign Israel was to experience its triumph and fulfilment as the centre of a great new world commonwealth in which peace and prosperity would flourish for all to enjoy. But till that day came their holy city, Jerusalem, and its temple were to remain standing free and inviolate as they had stood since the great days of David and Solomon as a sign that here God was going to do these great things.

Therefore when it all happened otherwise, and the inviolable city and temple were destroyed, it was hard for them to admit that God's future for them had been intended to involve humiliation as well as glory, exile and shame as well as security and prosperity. Could God really use a pagan like Nebuchadnezzar in any way as an instrument for their good or for their education? Were they really expected to believe that when they were in his brutal hands they were still in the hands of God?

It was especially hard for them to see their temple ruined and its vessels desecrated. They had bowed in awe before what they believed and felt to be the presence of God in that temple where these vessels were put to their exclusive holy use. Their tradition was full of stories which gave warning that no-one would ever be allowed even to lay profane hands on them without incurring dreadful and immediate retribution. But now a heathen monarch had dared, and had been allowed, to do precisely this!

They needed a new theology, and thinking it out was a slow process, involving heart-searching and controversy. The book of Daniel takes us into the world in which such problems were faced and thought through. But besides the problems of a new theology there were those of policy. They were now to live as a small minority group within an environment which they found sometimes threatening, sometimes friendly, but largely alien, to their culture and religious faith. A clergyman working among immigrants in a British city summed up the basic problem of such a group: how can we fit in without being swallowed?

As the chosen people of God they could never allow themselves to forget even there in Babylon the special promises of God about their future, made first to Abram, and often repeated and elaborated at crucial times in their history. These promises asserted that they were to inherit the land of Canaan. There they were to build a city and house for the living God; produce a line of kings culminating in a divine king; be blessed and become a blessing to all nations of the earth. Belief that this kind of thing was their national destiny had kept them together, and kept them apart from all other nations. But how was this destiny now to be fulfilled—under Nebuchadnezzar's rule, amidst the uncertainties of world conditions and upheavals of world history in these new times? Was there the least possibility of the 'promise' to Abram and the fathers now being realized at all? They had been uprooted from the 'land' to which it was attached. They were now scattered as a people into distant countries. Was it worth while still holding on to this tradition from their past and seeking to remain faithful to the call their fathers had so often heard? Could they dare expect the miracle of the great exodus from Egypt to be repeated in a new exodus from Babylon for them in their day?

Nebuchadnezzar: benevolence and despotism

The book of Daniel is from the start an extremely optimistic book. The writer is certain that from the moment the people of God were put in his power, Nebuchadnezzar himself, in every thought and whim of his mind, and in every plan and decree of his counsel, was closely and tightly under the control of the Lord. The emperor was raised up to preserve and not to destroy Israel. The intimation that he *placed the vessels in the treasury of his god* (verse 2) is meant to be read as a sign of this divine control. He might easily have destroyed them, or desecrated them (as did his reprobate successor) but under the hand of God, his decisions here, as ultimately in all other issues, are for the welfare and preservation of the people of God in the fulfilment of their destiny. The first four chapters of the book of Daniel have this as one of their main themes: to show how carefully God is at work controlling this man, Nebuchadnezzar, inspiring his decisions, over-ruling his folly, giving him his visions and dreams, making him mad when he will not co-operate, and returning him to sanity when he repents.

When he *commanded Ashpenaz, his chief eunuch, to bring some of the people of Israel, both of the royal family and of the nobility* (verse 3) in order to set up his school to teach the young Israelites *the letters and language of the Chaldeans* (verse 4), we find a change taking place in the man's policy and outlook. We can imagine him now as a man of war trying honestly to turn himself into a man of peace. His wars have brought out the worst in him, and in those who were with him. Wherever he led them, his armies worked havoc; burned houses and cities, levelled palaces and temples; killed, raped and plundered. Human victims were herded in droves, back to imperial Babylon.

But if war was that kind of business for him, peace was another kind of business, and the tasks of peace brought out another side of his complex personality. Babylon had to be replanned. A great new society had to be created, better and more stable than those that had fallen such an easy prey to his troops in the field, indeed, better than the past had ever known. He rose to this challenge too. The book of Daniel describes him as a man who liked building better than destroying. The first chapters of the book show him in the process of becoming a statesman who was both wise and moderate, shrewd and far-seeing. He now desires to take seriously his responsibility for the uplift and development of his enslaved populations. He seeks to exploit the social and human possibilities of his conquests, for he sees great potential value in all this human material he has brought to his Babylonian plains and cities. His programme centres not only on the enlightenment, uplift and unification of the captive peoples by Babylonization, he also wants to absorb as much as he can of the world's good into Babylon itself. These noble youths, for instance, *without blemish, handsome and skilful in all wisdom, endowed with knowledge, understanding learning, and competent to serve in the king's palace* (verse 4), could add splendour and effectiveness to his own Babylonian administration, and raise the standards of the local culture when he sent them out to the provinces.

Therefore we must interpret as a benevolent and enlightened gesture his decision to set up his Hebrew University near his palace. When he enrols the Hebrew youths in his three-year course of training in Babylonian wisdom, culture and statecraft, he does not conscript them by brute force, but entices them to matriculate by glowing descriptions of the privileges and prospects of the course. The *rich food* and royal *wine*, and the assurance of a job in the king's personal staff, are merely selected items of a prospectus of a college to which any free man in those days would rejoice to belong.

Of course the writer of the book does not gloss over the fact that Nebuchadnezzar still remains a despot, with tyrannical elements in his rule. But excuses can be pleaded for him. In the second chapter he lapses into a fit of uncontrollable anger, and threatens dreadful torture; but this lapse comes at a moment of psychological stress and is traced to his basic uncertainty about himself. The third chapter shows him rigid on the law-and-order issue and enraged at dissent; but he lived in an age when liberal and permissive views were unknown, and in a region where only dictatorship was known to work with large populations, and he had to exercise firm control over a potentially volcanic political situation. He honestly believed it necessary that the dissident few should be sacrificed for the well-being of all the others. The fourth chapter shows him puffed up for a moment or two with intense vanity at the thought of his astonishing achievement as the builder of Babylon. But he pays dearly for this lapse, and we finally see him ending his career, a humble, penitent, God-fearing man. Moreover, in the dream he was given by God in the second chapter, his empire is rated as having the worth of gold,[1] and of much higher quality than the succeeding world powers of the Middle East.

Perhaps then as we read the book we should think of him as something of a paternalist rather than a tyrant. He never doubted he knew best what was best for those he was destined to govern. His imperialistic ambitions were subtly blended and, he believed, sanctified with pure missionary zeal. But always his concern was rather to share privilege than merely to exercise power for its own sake.

As we read through the book we feel it was a tragedy that his earthly experiment failed so badly. He is shown to have been succeeded by a fool who spent his life dissipating what his predecessor had gathered and tearing down what he had built. His dynasty was succeeded by others of less worth, and in spite of the stories about it in this book, Babylon became a name later to be attached to the great and proud anti-Christian city that in the last days of the earth will tempt all peoples and nations to find their unity in having intercourse with what is vile and loathsome and doomed to fall, under the cover of its sham magnificence.[2]

Yet we are meant to understand, as we read the first chapters of our book, that these youths, under the rule of Nebuchadnezzar, faced an establishment which, even though foreign, offered promise of a worth-while career, under the leadership of one who by all human standards had great and praiseworthy qualities as a statesman.

The practical issues—co-operation or withdrawal?

We must try to imagine how the exiles faced the situation. When it came to deciding how to respond to Nebuchadnezzar's offers and plans for them, many of them were ready to try to settle down in the new Babylon comfortably and uncritically. No doubt some of them argued that those who lose their life find it, therefore in losing their own national identity they would be making their supreme national contribution to the great emerging cosmo-politan commonwealth. The world could be best served if in Babylon they forgot Zion. Moreover as individuals they may have seen that life in Babylon offered a measure of wealth and fulfilment unthinkable within a purely Judean milieu. When word

[1] Dn. 2:37, 38.   [2] Rev. 16:17—18:24.

34

went round of Nebuchadnezzar's search for recruits for his college, it is easy to picture how they would scramble for places for their children whom they readily called by new Babylonian names. They got rid of all their peculiar qualms about which kind of food was to be eaten and which kind shunned. The times were moving fast and they believed they were meant to move quickly with their times.

There must, however, have been those who reacted strongly the opposite way. The life of Israel never failed to produce people like the Rechabites[1] or the Zealots or the Pharisees,[2] sincere and dedicated, rigid in their adherence to the least detail of past tradition and deeply suspicious of all change even in cultural ways, always the first to refuse to bow down the knee to Baal. There were bound to be such among those carried into exile. We can imagine them standing firm in the belief that there could be no possible fraternization with the Babylonians over anything. They constantly looked on every attempt from the Babylonian side to achieve some measure of integration as an enticement to evil. They felt that under the paternalism of Nebuchadnezzar with his offers of education for leadership, his culturalization programmes and his plans to unify and bless all peoples under his rule, they were in greater danger than their forefathers had been under the fearful tyranny of Pharaoh in Egypt. Here was something essentially hostile in spirit to everything they had stood for as a nation—something that could destroy them more effectively by its enticements than the whip and torture had done in the Nile valley. They would rather have lived then than now. Their views were expressed perfectly in one of their later psalms:

> By the waters of Babylon, there we sat down and wept,
>   when we remembered Zion.
> On the willows there
>   we hung up our lyres.
> For there our captors
>   required of us songs,
> and our tormentors, mirth, saying,
>   'Sing us one of the songs of Zion!'
> How shall we sing the Lord's song
>   in a foreign land?[3]

[1] *Cf.* Je. 35.   [2] *Cf.* Mt. 15:1; 23:13–26.   [3] Ps. 137:1–4.

There were others among the captive community who felt that this attitude was too extreme. Some of them, like Daniel, were undoubtedly deeply influenced by a letter sent to them by the prophet Jeremiah not too long after they were taken into captivity:

> Build houses and live in them [he had written]; plant gardens and eat their produce. Take wives and have sons and daughters; take wives for your sons, and give your daughters in marriage, that they may bear sons and daughters; multiply there, and do not decrease. But seek the welfare of the city where I have sent you into exile, and pray to the Lord on its behalf, for in its welfare you will find your welfare.[2]

What exactly did this message mean? It is obvious that Jeremiah did not mean them to forget their inheritance or their destiny and lose their identity. No-one had ever resisted the watering down of the unique elements in their faith more than he had. No-one had been more of a nonconformist in his own way. To follow his advice, they would have to work out a way of settling down in Babylon for an extended period and of co-operating within the structures of its politics and the atmosphere of its culture, of winning if possible some of its prizes and rewards, of being loyal as its citizens and yet of retaining their communion with the God of their fathers and preserving all that was essential in their unique faith and witness.

The caretakers of the true Israel

A few young men are named in the book of Daniel because they found a way of fulfilling Jeremiah's advice of settling down and co-operating in Babylon and yet remaining always faithful to the tradition of their forefathers: *Daniel, Hananiah, Mishael and Azariah of the tribe of Judah* (verse 6).

They seem to have been all laymen. There is no mention of priest or even prophet as having a part to play in the religious movement represented here by these men. The whole structure of their community worship and sacrifice had been destroyed. We know that prophets continued to teach and preach during the exile, and it is certain that the community would have gathered

[1]Je. 29:4–7.

around teachers of the Word of God, who must have been trained in the prophetic or priestly tradition. Nevertheless, the book of Daniel reminds us that the continuity of a people's faith depends in the last resort on the reality of its lay witness and lay religion, rather than on the survival of its official clergy or its institutions.

There must have been some kind of community worship and teaching in the background of the lives of these young lay witnesses, and it is obvious from the first three chapters of Daniel that they practised group religion to some extent. They found strength in discussing, praying, studying and deciding together in the fellowship of the small 'cell' of believers. This helps to explain the strength of their solitary witness when they had to make such. It is almost impossible for anyone to maintain a vital faith in God and a strong witness to his ways in life, apart from the strength, wisdom, and fellowship that comes from within a community. Even one or two together can make such a strengthening community. When David was a lonely outlaw fleeing from Saul, it was a turning point in his life when 'Jonathan, Saul's son, rose, and went to David at Horesh, and strengthened his hand in God'.[1] Daniel at one point showed himself dependent on the courage and prayers of his companions.[2]

But it is obvious from the book that these lay witnesses were sometimes torn apart from each other and forced to make important decisions before God in life situations in which they were often isolated. The circumstances of their community at the time involved them in a great deal of lonely responsibility. Daniel himself oftens appears completely without companionship in his political struggles and his religious habits and experiences.[3] He found strength and assurance of forgiveness coming to him as he prayed alone.[4] Indeed he had to maintain his communion with God by the cultivation of what was obviously to him an intensely real personal devotional life of private prayer.[5]

The book of Daniel gives us the impression that what mattered most in the religious life of the exiles at this time was the discipline of the devotional and moral life around the law of God. This exile found that as he turned to the law of his God, studied it, meditated on it by himself or in the fellowship of the small group, devoted his life to its observance, he began to enter a new intensity of real personal relationship to the God who had given

[1] 1 Sa. 23 : 16.   [2] 2 : 17 f.   [3] 5 : 13 ff.; 6 : 10 ff.   [4] 9 : 20 ff.; 10 : 10 ff., 18.
[5] 6 : 10 ff.

the law for this purpose too. To turn thus to the law in exile was a sign of a personal return to the God who had so severely judged them as a nation.

But this required discipline. Daniel's personal religion gains its stability and strength from strict habits of devotion. As he adheres scrupulously to the law it becomes a means of blessing to him.

Throughout the book, Daniel appears as outstanding in several different roles. He is unforgettable because of his dreams and apocalyptic visions of the future which have fired the imagination and guided the thoughts of generations of devout students of the Bible. The wisdom and tact with which he deals pastorally and diplomatically with the situations that come to pass in the court world of his time force us to place him along with Joseph as one of the great 'wise men' of history. He is remarkable as a model of living personal piety and upright behaviour and loyal adherence to tradition. But he appears clearly in the first four chapters of the book as the leader of a significant group of men through whose simple, quiet, determined acts of protest and non-co-operation the faith and tradition of at least a section of the nation was kept distinct and vigorous for a generation and more. Indeed the implication of the book is that in this role he played an important part in keeping the true faith alive at a time of great testing.

Though it was four of them who took such an effective stand, they were obviously under the leadership of this one outstanding and therefore rather solitary individual. He was outstanding and influential simply because before he made a decision he waited for no-one else except God, and refused to conform to what others placed like him were lining up meekly to do. Can this not be a challenge to us today? Instead of our always being moved around by our environment, might it not be our responsibility to move our environment? Instead of having the direction of our lives dictated by social, community and even ecclesiastical pressure, do we not, each of us, have a very heavy and quite individual responsibility to listen for ourselves to the voice of God, plan our own thing without seeking to know how others are going to plan, and decide without always waiting to know how others are going jump? This was what Abram did, and what Moses did. It was what Elijah had to do, alone, even though there were seven thousand others thinking like himself.[1] It was the line Joshua was pleading

[1] 1 Ki. 17:1; 19:10, 18.

38

with each of his hearers to take in his great sermon ending: 'Choose this day whom you will serve, . . . but as for me and my house, we will serve the Lord.' [1]

The Old Testament time and again, by appeal and example, calls on the individual to stand firm where others are compromising and drifting.[2] The New Testament warns us against drifting with and conforming to the world[3] as seriously as the Old warns us against following the 'multitude' into evil.[4] It is important for us never to forget that Jesus himself in his day took a stand against accepted ways and patterns, and gathered round himself a band of others to be with him in his mission. The pattern that he followed is there in the life of Daniel.

Yes and no!

Daniel and his companions eagerly grasped the privileges offered them within the school opened by Nebuchadnezzar. Their policy, as we see them in this book, was to co-operate, but without compromise. This meant saying Yes! to the challenges and invitations of Babylonian life. It meant facing up in a realistic way to the situation around them with its need for action, witness and love from the people of God. Their views are indeed so 'broad' that they do not object to being given Babylonian *names* instead of their own (verse 7). They readily take on top jobs in the pagan imperial administration.[5] Daniel at the height of his success can even accept without protest an offering of incense, which looked suspiciously like worship, from Nebuchadnezzar.[6]

Yet while they make such concessions, they do so always with such a spirit of detachment that at any point the answer No! could be given, no matter at what cost, loudly and clearly.[7] They remain inner strangers to the life and culture in which they are outwardly and fully involved. They never sacrifice their inward conviction that they belong body and soul to a kingdom other than that of Babylon. They try, moreover, never to lose touch with the strange impelling Word of God which comes to them as they meet together to read, study their Scriptures and pray that they might share the same vision and hope as had inspired their nation's kings, prophets and wise men. They discipline their lives and minds to ensure that they will always

[1]Jos. 24:15.   [2]*E.g.* Ps. 1.   [3]Rom. 12:2.   [4]Ex. 23:2.   [5]1:19; 2:49.
[6]2:46.   [7]3:18; 6:10.

remain open to hear what this Word has to say to them in the midst of the literal Babel of other voices all around them. Their aim in accepting their education in Nebuchadnezzar's school is certainly to *stand before the king* (verses 5, 19), but they are determined to do this not as Babylonians but as dedicated Israelites. Therefore, while they settle down to Babylonian life they remain always aware that in all their duties and temptations they are being put to the test, not by Nebuchadnezzar, but by the God of Abraham, Isaac and Jacob, whose they are and whom they must serve and love before anything else. They remain deeply convinced that their future as a nation, and therefore the future of other nations, depends on their remaining separate, and on their ultimately going back home across the deserts to Jerusalem to take up again a national life of their own.

They are, therefore, prepared to serve Babylon, to build up its society and shape its history, but never to the extent of sacrificing their own national history for that of Babylon. They are prepared to pay tribute to Nebuchadnezzar, but never to the extent of lessening their own commitment to the God of their fathers. They find it neither impossible nor even difficult to co-operate without coming to the point of violating their conscience in its loyalty to the Word of God. They even enjoy their Babylonian life—but they are always ready to resist when the interests of Babylon clash with the interests of the kingdom of God, and they can speak the word No! always clearly and decisively, if politely.

The first encounter

The early chapters of the book of Daniel contain memorable incidents in which we clearly hear their No! spoken dramatically and publicly. Three of them said it when they were threatened with the burning fiery furnace if they did not bow down to Nebuchadnezzar's image.[1] Daniel said it when he knew he was threatened with being thrown to the lions if he went on praying to his God.[2] But their resistance begins much earlier in a rather quiet and undramatic interview which took place within the privacy of the office of the chief of the eunuchs, whose job seems to have been very like that of the principal, even dean of students, in a modern college. A decision was made there and then that took as much determined courage and put their lives at as much risk as

[1] 3:16–18.   [2] 6:10.

their later more dramatic exploits. It can be affirmed that if this first decision had not been made there would later have been no resistance at all to the burning fiery furnace or to the threat of being cast into the lion's den. Within the context of the whole of Scripture Daniel's decision not to eat the king's rich food is meant to be compared in importance with Abraham's decision to leave his homeland in obedience to the word of God,[1] or with Moses' decision at the burning bush to accept at last his responsibility to lead his people out of bondage.[2] All these three great decisions arose from the same deep inner conviction at the time of their being made, and in each case they were decisions fraught with destiny.

In that quiet undramatic interview with Ashpenaz, Daniel was as powerfully under divine inspiration and guidance as any of his apparently far greater predecessors at earlier turning-points in the history of Israel, and this inspiration continued with him as he devoted his whole mind and life to the quiet and steady career of faithfulness and endurance which seemed to be opening out before him. It is because he was basically a man of ordinary human stature and build, whose secret is simply obedience and loyalty, that he is portrayed here as a model and source of inspiration for future generations.

The issue, and the drawing of the line

In Daniel's time, the danger to his own nation which had to be faced by its leaders was that of drifting into complete conformity with the customs and traditions of the surrounding world, thus altering entirely its historical course and direction, and losing sight of the purposes for which God had brought it into existence. For men placed as Daniel was placed, and thinking as Daniel did, felt that they could not serve God with a clear conscience unless a line was drawn somewhere, and a firm stand taken at certain points. Some undeviating principles of conduct and belief for that day had to be defined and established, and, as we have seen, adherence to these established principles had to become a matter of conscience for each individual. Little did Daniel realize that he was the custodian of his national traditions and fortunes to such an extent!

The question was: where was the line to be drawn? Where was

[1]Gn. 12:1 ff.   [2]Ex. 3:1 ff.

compromise to be possible, where was it to become impossible? Daniel was convinced that under the circumstances of the exile there could be no compromise with the traditional food laws. Possibly he felt that the abolition of the food laws would open the door to mixed marriages and religious and financial compromise. At any rate, at this point, he felt that the whole distinctive existence of his nation depended on this outward sign of difference and separation. He accordingly made it a matter of conscience and confession. He believed that faithfulness even in observing outward regulations mattered, for what was truly and uniquely inward was subtly dependent on what was outward.

Daniel resolved that he would not defile himself with the king's rich food, or with the wine which he drank; therefore he asked the chief of the eunuchs to allow him not to defile himself (verse 8). Certainly it sounds rather superstitious. What form of real contamination could have come through mere eating and drinking? Is it not also far too legalistic? Did not Jesus condemn the whole outlook when he said, 'There is nothing outside a man which by going into him can defile him; but the things which come out of a man are what defile him'?[1]

But under certain circumstances issues that otherwise might be thought trivial can become matters of first importance. The wearing of a little emblem, the giving of a salute, the singing of a short liberation song, however poor the tune or the words, can inspire heroic resistance or incite demonic opposition. We have just passed through a time in western cultural history when the length of a boy's hair could assume such symbolic importance that it became an issue almost of life and death within a home. And under the providence and blessing of God, trivial acts such as the distribution of bread and wine amongst a Christian congregation or the use of a little water in an act of baptism can become acts of surpassing significance and power. Under the circumstances of the exile Daniel felt that a hopeless drift could be halted only by standing firm on the law, even in matters which at other times might seem inconsequential and strange.

Daniel's concern was that he should *not defile himself*. This does not mean that he believed that literally some material pollution could come to him through physically eating forbidden food, and that this could cause at the same time some moral taint on his soul. His thinking followed quite another line. He simply

[1]Mk. 7:15.

believed that faith in God and the forgiveness of God had made him clean. This was a cleansing from the idolatry of the surrounding world, and the moral pollution that accompanied it. It meant a call to a new and different life. These food laws and other customs that kept him separate were to him the sign and symbol of this inner cleansing. But if he compromised on these laws and allowed these signs of separation which safeguarded his distinctive inner attitude to be removed, then inevitably he would allow himself to be drawn back and to become immersed in the customs from which he had been cleansed, and he would no longer be fully useful as a distinctive instrument for God's use.

A model for today?

It is significant that Daniel in his attitude on this issue became a model for the behaviour of many loyal Jews at the time when they were being persecuted under Antiochus Epiphanes in the second century BC. Antiochus himself recognized that if he was to succeed in destroying the distinctive witness of the Jewish community and absorb them into his Hellenistic culture, he would have to get them to give up among other things the distinctive eating customs that kept them so much apart. In his attempt to break down Jewish resistance at this point he passed laws condemning Jewish ceremonial regulations in matters of food and commanding conformity to normal eating practices. The matter became a confessional issue, a test as to whether or not one was loyal to the whole Jewish tradition, and prepared to fight and die for its preservation. The contemporary writings tell us that many Jews refused to 'defile themselves', and chose to die rather than give way on this issue. Many scholars believe that the book of Daniel was written up and issued at this time by some editor from the circles of the faithful, to help to inspire and sustain the movement of resistance to Antiochus.

Today a situation is arising in many parts of the western world similar to that which then confronted Daniel. As Christians we are bound often to feel the same tension he felt as we face around us a world rapidly changing in its ethical and religious outlook and permitted customs. The current of change is so powerful that it tends to swallow up in itself anything that is not strongly committed to another viewpoint. Undoubtedly we have to make some concessions to change. We cannot remain exactly where we were a generation ago. Yet the direction of the prevalent changes are often so radically alien to our Christian way that we cannot possibly follow it totally without losing our power to witness clearly to what we believe is the nature of God and the gospel, and the meaning of life on earth.

Therefore in a situation where a measure of change is inevitable, we have to ask where are we to draw the line, say our No!, and take a firm stand. Though questions of eating and drinking are not now in our Christian tradition points of confession and separation for us as they were for Daniel, there are nevertheless always the things that 'defile' us too as decidedly as these did in the days of the exile. The purpose of the life, death and teaching of Christ was to cleanse mankind and liberate them from customs and ways that corrupt individual men and women morally and spiritually and that pollute community life. He himself pleaded with his followers to cut out of their lives attitudes and habits that defile the heart and mind:

> If your right eye causes you to sin, pluck it out and throw it away; it is better that you lose one of your members than that your whole body should be thrown into hell. And if your right hand causes you to sin, cut if off and throw it away; it is better that you lose one of your members than that your whole body go into hell.[1]

The New Testament time and again brings us back to the question raised by Jesus in these words, warning us not to forget our cleansing,[2] and to 'hate what is evil'.[3] To encourage and warn us, the cross is held out as the price he paid that we might be made and kept clean and whole.

But his work is negated and his pleas are unheeded if we conform carelessly to whatever now becomes the 'done thing' in the permissive moods that sweep our society into moral and spiritual change. The new spirit of the age is not always that of Christ. We are bound to come to a point where we feel that Christ died to cleanse us from the defilement of this way of life held before us and therefore we cannot go any further and keep faith with our God. There is no doubt that understood in this way there is a 'dirt' in certain forms of political activity, in certain aspects of the entertainment and publishing world, in certain of the news

[1]Mt. 5:29, 30. [2]E.g. 1 Cor. 6:9-11; 2 Pet. 1:5-9. [3]Rom. 12:9.

media, that we must not defile ourselves by touching. Moreover many of the things in life that have proved stable and healthy both to ourselves and to generations before us—in marriage and family life for instance—can be preserved only if we draw the line somewhere and learn to re-echo this No! We must not underestimate the importance of the stand we may be being called upon to take. When Daniel made his quiet decision to say his No! he cannot have realized that he was playing a part of such great significance in the re-orientation of his nation's life towards finding again its true place in the service of God.

The vow and the appeal

It is important to note that the issue was brought to a head and was pressed convincingly, and the protest gained its full effect, simply because Daniel had, through a previous vow, decided to make it always a matter of undeviating principle. The Authorized Version reflects the Hebrew more literally when it records that Daniel *purposed in his heart* (verse 8) that he would not compromise on the issue. Therefore Daniel left nothing open for an existential decision on the spur of the moment.

We are thus meant to understand that his course of action was carefully thought out and determined beforehand under the illumination and wisdom given to him by the Spirit of God. We can well believe that through prayer with mind and heart he sought God's guidance on how the life of faith was to be lived out in his day and generation. He came to certain conclusions, believed his prayer was answered, and bound himself by a solemn vow to keep his decisions. We can even imagine him to have passed through a deeply felt religious experience as he made such a vow. At any rate he made his behaviour in these issues a matter of principle. Such decisions were too important to be left to the moral inspiration of the moment when the matter was raised. Indeed, he chose himself to raise the issue in his own time and place, to declare what he believed, and to indicate what he was going to do. This took immense courage on his part. He would not have been able to summon the courage had he not already found himself pledged through the vow.

His example challenges us to think again about the value of pledging ourselves to God through a vow and even of acting at times on principles. We tend to decry such behaviour, and we stress the fact that in the intricacies and realities of our ethical situation sometimes action 'on principle' becomes inadequate. It is true that ethical principles which have come down to us from past generations require always to be re-examined and sometimes discarded. The nature of each concrete situation as it occurs before us on our journey through life has to be taken into account in our decisions about how to respond and what to do. But in all this, rules and principles to which we have been led to commit ourselves also matter. So does rational thinking beforehand about such principles and rules. If we are serious in the game we too will have our moments for making our vows.

We have to note how gently, courteously, and therefore how appealingly Daniel raised the issues with Ashpenaz, choosing the place and the moment, and trying to win him by wisdom and tact (verses 8ff.). He raised no suspicion that he expected his overseer to adopt some new or extreme outlook. All he asked on the part of his hearer was an attempt to understand the force of the tradition and conviction under which he was appealing. He showed deference. It is implied in the text that he even asked for *compassion* (verse 9). He begged to be given the benefit of trial by result. He did it quietly and humbly and God added all the finishing touches that were necessary.

Of course his options were few. When they wanted to protest they did not in those days carry placards, conduct marches or lie down in awkward places. No-one would have dreamed of calling anyone in authority a 'pig'. But the story seems to imply that when people have right on their side, take pains to make their witness clear and to present their case as rationally and logically and courteously as possible, then they follow the path of true wisdom and leave room for God to enter the situation and to work as he wills.

God takes over

The book of Daniel is not simply about the witness and stand of a small brave group within an alien civilization and in an evil age. It is about how God himself works in such circumstances. It is written chiefly to show us how he comes into people's lives and circumstances whether they are believers or unbelievers, how, when events seem to be going against his purposes, he intervenes and alters things to make them go his way, how he brings to destruction and death whatever and whomever he wills, and raises up from destruction and death whatever and whomever he wills.[1]

The writer of the book is especially interested in the way he miraculously and meticulously works within people's inward thoughts and feelings, changing their intentions, hearts and plans—and thus altering history. Whether they are awake or asleep it does not matter. God works in the subconscious mind-sphere as powerfully as he does in the conscious mind, ultimately bringing up dreams or visions of deep significance for their decisions and destiny.[2]

But chiefly he works while people are awake and alert, putting new thoughts in their brains and subtly directing their preferences one way or another. He does this kind of thing sometimes while they are thinking quietly by themselves about life and history, sometimes while they are praying, sometimes while they are giving interviews or making decrees in council or going about other kinds of business. He rules history by controlling the thoughts and appetites of lions as well as men![3]

Thus affairs in Babylon are made to work out in favour of God's people and for the fulfillment of God's purposes, not by means of any one spectacular intervention by God in history, but by means of a series of decisions taken quietly within the routine business of the administration of the Babylonian civil service. *And God gave Daniel favour and compassion in the sight of the chief of the eunuchs; . . . so he hearkened to them in this matter* (verses 9, 14).

Of course the God who is witnessed to in the book of Daniel can also work spectacular miracles in the physical realm. The fire does not scorch the three young martyrs,[4] and in the chapter before us we have a miracle no less wonderful: *At the end of ten days it was seen that they were better in appearance and fatter in flesh than all the youths who are the king's rich food* (verse 15).

But such remarkable physical miracles are meant to be understood as signs that much more remarkable miracles are being worked below the surface of human affairs, as the Babylonian bureaucrats drink their morning coffee and hold their committee meetings, and as the young students whose future is at stake make up their minds on policy and ethics. Daniel's resolve in his heart to say No! was no less miraculous a work of God than his survival in the lions' den. 'You cannot tell by observation', said

---

[1] *Cf.* 2:20–22; 3:28; 6:26, 27.   [2] *Cf.* 2:1; 4:5.
[3] 1:19; 2:25 ff., 46; 3:24; 6:22.   [4] *Cf.* 3:24 ff.

Jesus, 'when the kingdom of God comes.'[1]

The chapter ends with a remark about the staying power of this man Daniel: *Daniel continued until the first year of King Cyrus* (verse 21). He represents what is left of the people of God after the collapse of the temple and the eclipse of the royal line of David. Though these things have collapsed, nothing has been able to destroy the individual who looks for God and his promises and obeys his law. And it is this man who outlasts the Babylonian and Median empires and outlives two or three royal dynasties.

[1]Lk. 17:20 NEB.

Daniel 2
The stone and the shattered kingdoms

Crisis in palace and city

IN the second year of the reign of Nebuchadnezzar, Nebuchad-nezzar had dreams; and his spirit was troubled, and his sleep left him (verse 1).

Why should Nebuchadnezzar have dreamed such dreams? Nothing on earth could present any real threat to his security. He had enormous power and wealth. Popular, respected, feared his word was never questioned nor his will disputed. His armies in the field had just won some of their greatest successes. Yet night after night it happened—this dream! Day after day he woke up haunted by an ever-vague yet ever-growing suspicion that his personal well-being and the security of his kingdom were threatened by something beyond his control, something from beyond the visible sphere of this world. He felt increasingly insecure. As his uneasiness grew, his sense of frustration and his anger also grew.

He was maddened to discover that not one of his wise men, for whose services he paid handsomely, could probe deep enough to explain the real cause of his mental and emotional exhaustion and imbalance, and bring to light what was lurking in his subconscious mind. He flourished money in the eyes of his magicians, astrologers and philosophers. '*If you show the dream and its interpretation,*' he cried, '*you shall receive from me gifts and rewards and great honour*' (verse 6). And in case his bribery did not work, he uttered the ultimate threat: '*If you do not make known to me the dream and its interpretation, you shall be torn limb from limb, and your houses shall be laid in ruins*' (verse 5).

All to no avail! Here was something that, with all his power and influence in the arts of Babylon, Nebuchadnezzar could not master. Here was something that belonged to a realm in which his beck and call were not given the least priority. It was this very fact that increased his sense of frustration and anger to an even more serious pitch.

His experiences began to change him. He indulged more frequently than ever before in morose fits of anger and gloom, and suspected everyone. He accused his counsellors of conspiracy to deceive and torment him (verse 8). The atmosphere of his court changed too. His former friends began to walk in terror. We can imagine his own family filled with distress and asking what these dreams could be that were now making such a monster out of one who had been so warm-hearted and human. Things moved to a crisis when he gave orders to Arioch for a blood bath involving all his wise men (verses 12ff.).

Perhaps we can recognize in Nebuchadnezzar a prototype of many others who have been in politics. Reinhold Neibuhr is right in finding this sense of insecurity, this anxiety complex at the root of much of our modern political tyranny. The lust for power in man, he finds, is prompted by a 'darkly conscious realization' of the insecurity of his existence. 'Man is tempted by the basic insecurity of human existence to make himself doubly secure',[1] and so he grasps after position, fame, wealth and power. But the more he attains and the higher he climbs, the more basically insecure he feels his position, for the more terrible his fall could be. Therefore the more he attains, the more desperately and anxiously he is driven to strive to attain. And so we have the vicious circle which produces the modern dictator, and which forces the dictator in his rule to become more and more harsh, brutal, angry and suspicious. And we have racial and social minorities driven to become more and more irrational and oppressive in the use of power while it is in their hands, because of a fearful sense of sheer weakness in face of the inevitably crushing course events must take some time in the future.

We need not, however, confine ourselves to tyrants or political groups when we seek modern examples of what the Bible typifies for us in Nebuchadnezzar with his uneasy dreams. He helps us also to explain some of our individual and domestic tragedies. He is an example of the deep-hidden sense of insecurity that can drive

[1]R. Niebuhr, *The Nature and Destiny of Man*, I (Nisbet 1944), pp. 201–203.

a man to drink, to ever-unsatisfied acquisitiveness, to the inordinate pursuit of pleasure, to irrational anger, to behaviour towards friends and family that is strange and ominous.

Ultimate questions

Of course, mixed up somehow with all Nebuchadnezzar's subconscious questions about the stability of his empire and house-building were all the other questions—the common ultimate questions raised every day by ordinary people in modest positions with not too much wealth and power, who sometimes become deeply aware of their tragic finitude and go through what a modern theologian calls the 'shock of possible non-being'. What is the purpose of life and existence? Where does it tend and where will it end? Why does there come to me, too, at the very best and highest moments of my life, the strange disturbing thought that even this might be the material of tragedy? Why is so much that is good and beautiful marked so deeply and indelibly with clear signs of instability and frailty? Even Solomon, after proving his heart with mirth and pleasure, wine and wisdom, after building all his great works and planting his pleasure gardens, after marshalling and reviewing his servants, maidens and cattle, and admiring his treasures to the accompaniment of his singers and music, could look from the height of his greatness at all the work that his hands had wrought, only to find that 'behold, all was vanity and a striving after wind, and there was nothing to be gained under the sun'.[1]

It is significant that Nebuchadnezzar at this crisis in his life cries out not merely to be told the interpretation of a dream that he himself knows to arise out of the deep recesses of his own subconscious mind, but to be told the very dream itself. It reminds us that when we come to be faced with the same kind of ultimate problems as were so troubling him in his day, we too have nothing within the world of our own thought, conscious or subconscious, be it a dream or a question or a tentative philosophy of life, that can lead us even towards the light of the final answer that our heart cries out for. We cannot raise the ultimate questions for this ultimate answer. All the light and wisdom we seek must come from a source quite other than ourselves, and we need around us not only those who are experts on answering human questions

[1]Ec. 2:1–11.

but also those who can put us in touch with the Wisdom and the Word that is entirely from beyond.

Daniel the mediator

It is interesting to compare Daniel's reaction to the situation facing him in the first chapter, with his response when he now hears of Nebuchadnezzar's problem and threats (verses 14–16). There he said No! clearly and decisively: he will neither conform nor participate. Here, however, he says Yes! just as clearly and decisively. He accepts his involvement in this acute and tragic human situation, and in the most practical way he gives himself to respond to and answer this desperate *cri de coeur* and to try to do something positive for those around him.

If this was the case with Daniel in his world, might it not happen so with us in our world? We sometimes undertake too readily, too neatly, to prescribe the kind of behaviour that we expect others and ourselves to have to follow in serving Christ. We tend sometimes even to make words like 'involvement' and 'separation' become simple and exclusive central principles of conduct. Certainly, as we have already seen,[1] defined principles and rules can help us at times to keep steadily and strongly on a certain course. Moreover rules are so necessary for our guidance that God has given us an unforgettable, simply-stated code of strong clear commandments for us always to listen to with fear and trembling. But the one whose voice we are listening for in our ethical decisions, and whose example we always have to follow, was himself infinitely separate from sinners,[2] and yet at the same time deeply and passionately involved with life and sinners too. In differing circumstances for us there may be times when we know ourselves called to express our witness to him in differing ways.

The main point in the story is that Daniel at this moment becomes a key man. He alone is able to act decisively and shrewdly where others are hopelessly incapable and benumbed. By an act of solitary leadership he is able to prevent the disaster threatening both Nebuchadnezzar and his counsellors. He steps into the breach, and finds that God gives him the wisdom and power to control the situation. All this is meant to be understood by the reader as the fulfilment of the promise of God that, through the

[1]See above, pp. 45f.   [2]Heb. 7:26.

descendants of Abraham, even the pagans shall be blessed.[1] His motives are certainly mixed. The personal threat to his own safety compels him to take this action to save his own life and those of his friends. But he is acting not simply for himself but out of faith in God whom he knows to be at work in the situation, and though he may have been only dimly conscious of the full significance of what was happening, he must have felt himself as certain now of his divine calling to be this particular witness to the power of God in this particular way, as he was of his calling to protest against unclean food.

No doubt he reacts to the situation around him differently from all the other religious men of Babylon because he alone is in touch with a God who cares and works practically and marvellously. This is why at this moment he has to become involved rather than remain separate. Indeed it is because he is in touch with the God of Israel that he feels constrained to serve not only the people of Israel, but the pagan empire Babylon. For the God of Israel cares for this heathen emperor and his peace of mind, cares too, even about the fate of that handful of poor, lost, so-called 'wise men' who were little more than a pack of deluded wizards. The light God had shed on Israel for centuries past is now beginning to fall on such as Nebuchadnezzar and his magicians.

Daniel's bearing, as he faces the political crisis in Babylon and fulfills his mediating task, presents two other highly contrasting aspects. He acts with extreme circumspection and prudence. He is cautious. There is not a trace of superficial confidence. He is careful not to give offence. There is no brash attempt at evangelism. All the time he is in fear and trembling, and, up to the moment when the revelation of the mystery dawns on him, his agony piles up. He pleads earnestly with his three companions not to let him or the cause of God down by ceasing to pray as he seeks *the mercy of heaven concerning this mystery* (verses 17, 18). When the answer to this prayer comes, he breaks out spontaneously into humble and astonished thanksgiving (verse 20). The answer comes only just in time. The anxious tension is maintained till the last possible moment and Arioch has to rush quickly to the mentally deranged king to tell him that all is now well.

Throughout this situation, though he himself has seen no possible way open, Daniel has acted with complete confidence

[1] *Cf.* Gn. 12 : 1, 2, *etc.*

that God would give him, at the moment of need, wisdom to solve any problem, and strength to face up to any threat. He believed that, though he himself at the beginning saw no possible way through the dilemmas and complexities of the situation, yet all the time God had a way and a solution for everything; and surely God would make the way clear even at the moment of direst perplexity. He has been certain that in the crisis he and his friends would be able to pray as none of the others involved knew how, to a God who would never fail. He has gone about the task confident that he was to be an agent of a true miracle. Though he is weak and knows nothing, this man is nevertheless strong and knows everything because he is trusting the living God.

The mystery of the king's dream

In a *vision of the night* (verse 19) the *mystery* or secret of the king's dream was revealed to Daniel. This means that in some way or other he began to receive a new understanding of the plans, purposes and affairs of God on earth that are deeply concealed from human wisdom. It means too that he began to receive some clue as to how he himself and Nebuchadnezzar with his dream were involved in the unfolding and working out of this purpose. There can be no doubt as we read through the chapter from the beginning that the mystery was about how God changes *times and seasons, removes kings and sets up kings* (verse 21) and thus makes history serve his will, glory and love.

Later, Daniel, often by himself and often in prayer,[1] receives many more 'revelations' of the course things are to take as history moves towards its end. Sometimes specific numbers of years are given to define the length of intervals of time, yet these numbers are used so ambiguously and mysteriously that to sort things out exactly becomes tantalizingly impossible. Sometimes the revelation is given through the use of weird shapes and strange symbols. Nebuchadnezzar's dream is the first of these symbolic visions about this mystery, and it helps us to understand all the rest. It gives us simply a preliminary sketch of one aspect of the whole course of history as it culminates in the kingdom of God. This dream embodies the first vague yet exciting and satisfying revelation to Daniel of the way God is yet going to fulfil the promise given to Abraham[2] from the beginning.

[1] *E.g.* 7:1 ff.; 8:1 ff.; 9:24 ff.; 11:1 ff. [2] Gn. 12:1 ff.

In seeking from God an understanding of the mystery, Daniel was simply following many of his predecessors, the prophets. They themselves[1] had known that as history unfolded the promise, God would seek faithfully to fulfil his part of the covenant given so freely to Abraham[2] and entered into again at Sinai,[3] and they held on to their belief in the promises about the establishment of the throne of David for ever.[4] Their call to their ministry involved the task of keeping the promises before the people, recalling them to their part in fulfilling them, and trying to explain how God was going to work around them in order to do his part, and of how the wonder of his work would be gloriously revealed in the 'latter days'. These same prophets, like Daniel in this chapter, were given partial insights into this mystery, and had clothed these in memorable oracles.[5]

But Daniel at this time was in a position to discover with a clarity hitherto not known in Israel exactly how God was at work with this purpose, not only in Israel's own thoughts and life but also here and there in the surrounding pagan world, even in Babylon, and especially in the dream life of the emperor of Babylon. There had been early hints of God's readiness to reveal the mystery of his purposes to those outside his covenant people,[6] but on the whole the great prophets had felt that when God had important things to do and say he would intimate them to the prophets of Israel.[7] Daniel, then, outstandingly, indulges in a remarkably daring flight of thought. He identified the *mystery* (verse 18) with the hidden content of the king's dream or the *king's matter* (verse 23). He therefore approached the whole problem in the firm belief that this distraught Gentile was being given some deep insight by the God of Israel into the ultimate future of mankind, and both in his dreams and in his awakened mind he was genuinely trying, in his own way, to grapple with the same problem as had for centuries burdened the prophets and the great men of Israel. In pleading with his companions to help him to understand what was going on in Nebuchadnezzar's mind he was hoping to discover something vital and new with which to enrich the traditions of his own nation as it, too, faced its future.

For his knowledge and understanding of the revelation of this mystery Daniel insisted that he was dependent entirely on divine

---

[1]See above, p. 23.   [2]Gn. 15, 17.   [3]Ex. 19 ff.   [4]2 Sa. 7:16.
[5]Je. 31:1 ff.; Is. 9:1 ff.; Am. 9:11 ff.; Mi. 4:11 ff.; Joel 2:28 ff.
[6]*E.g.* Gn. 12:17 ff.; Nu. 22 ff.   [7]Am. 3:7; though *cf.* Is. 45:1 ff.

inspiration. He pleads with his companions for prayer for divine help as his mind tries to probe it (verse 18), and as he seeks later to speak about it and explain it to the king (verses 27ff.), he acknowledges that God himself alone *gives wisdom to the wise and knowledge to those who have understanding; he reveals deep and mysterious things; he knows what is in the darkness, and the light dwells with him* (verses 21, 22).

No wise men, enchanters, magicians or astrologers can give the slightest help (verse 27) towards the understanding Daniel is seeking. Nor can any amount of human research, group consultation, or acuteness in understanding the ordinary forces that make for change within secular society. Daniel is conscious all through that in seeking this 'understanding', what he desires is pure light from beyond, a seeing and comprehending that is sheer miracle and that arises through fellowship with the God who himself sees things from above. His only hope of ever attaining such understanding lies in admitting that he has come to the end of all the resources of his own mind, and in uttering the prayer of a blind man for the miracle of seeing.

The proclamation of the kingdom of God

As soon as the mystery was revealed to him, Daniel felt confident that this was what Nebuchadnezzar had been seeing in some form in his dream. In explaining it to the king he tried to interpret the whole matter in terms that Nebuchadnezzar would understand. He describes a statue of huge dimensions (verses 31ff.), with *head of gold, breast and arms of silver, belly and thighs of bronze.* It impresses the viewer with its strength and solidity, its terrifying appearance, until, that is, its *feet* are seen to be made merely of a weak and utterly valueless mixture of *iron* and *clay*. The whole thing is unstable. It dare not even try to move one inch. But it was not mainly and finally the weakness of the legs and feet that caused the fall of this great symbol of human achievement in history: *As you looked, a stone was cut out by no human hand, and it smote the image on its feet of iron and clay, and broke them in pieces; then the iron, the clay, the bronze, the silver, and the gold, all together were broken in pieces, and became like the chaff of the summer threshing floors; and the wind carried them away, so that not a trace of them could be found* (verses 34f.). This end was far more dramatic and unexpected than the mere development of feet of clay could ever bring about, for the whole great statue was pulverized into fine dust by the impact of the stone as if by a nuclear explosion, and *the stone that struck the image became a great mountain and filled the whole earth* (verse 35).

Daniel was brutally frank in explaining the meaning of the dream to the king. The time remaining to the empire he was building was now comparatively short. It would, of course, go through its development in the process of history. It would help to give place and shape to three or four other empires, each in its own way impressive and mighty. But this development itself would ultimately reveal that all the greatness and magnificence of the structure was resting on feet of crumbling clay that could not bear it for long. The end, however, would come not because there were these feet of clay, but because the whole structure stood in the way and blocked the progress of another kingdom that must come and fill the future. It was because this future kingdom was approaching, and because its triumph was inevitable, that Nebuchadnezzar's empire and dynasty would be broken up.

When we study the king's dream as Daniel related it to him, we can see that at this point the explanation of the mystery of how human history was going to unfold was cast into a form that would be easily understandable, both to King Nebuchadnezzar with his pagan background and to Daniel and others around him living in their own tradition. There was a tradition current in the world of his day that human history would consist of four great ages, that each succeeding one would be less happy than the preceding, and that each could be characterized by a series of metals, each one in the series becoming more debased than the preceding one. No doubt Nebuchadnezzar knew this myth which certainly embodied a great truth of human experience, and he readily got the message for himself.

But two other great pictures from the past may have been in Daniel's mind as his vision took its final shape and its meaning dawned on his mind. One, of course, was the story of David slaying Goliath—the great Philistine who stood so mockingly in the way of the progress of the people of God in order to block the fulfilment of God's purpose to give them fully the land they had begun to conquer.[1] Centuries later this great story is being picked up and retold to assure not only the people of God, but others as well, that no earthly power should dare to stand thus in the way of

[1] Sa. 17:31 ff.

God's people. The other is the vision of Isaiah and Micah of how the mountain of the house of the Lord shall be established above all other hills, and all nations shall go to it for guidance and fellowship.[1]

The details of the image

Daniel does not explain in detail which metal stands for which forthcoming empire in the earthly succession of kingdoms symbolized in the image. He seems simply to suggest that four outstanding and different empires will run their course before the kingdom of God finally enters the world with new dynamic power as the deciding factor in history. The message is repeated in chapter 7 where the course of history is represented by four successive beasts instead of by four descending sections of a statue. Since verse 44 of the present chapter states that in the day of the final one of the four empires *the God of heaven will set up a kingdom which shall never be destroyed*, many commentators have suggested that this must refer to the birth, death and resurrection of Jesus in the Roman era, and that the empires referred to are therefore: (1) Babylonian, (2) Medo-Persian, (3) Greek, (4) Roman. But many modern scholars think that what was referred to in verse 44 was expected by the writer to take place around the era of Antiochus Epiphanes (175–163 BC) in the age of Greece. Others think that verse 44 refers to the second coming of Christ at the end of all ages. Those who take such views make up slightly different lists of the succession of kingdoms. We can at least reserve our final judgment till we have studied the whole book, especially chapter 7. Moreover we must remember that what was important in Daniel's mind as he spoke about the vision was not to define his four empires exactly, but to fix Nebuchadnezzar's mind on the inevitability of the coming and triumph of the kingdom of God.

The stone from the mountain

Of the meaning of the stone we can have no doubt. Christ's is the kingdom *cut from a mountain by no human hand* (verses 34, 45), which will come, breaking into history and altering history, bringing devastating judgment on all that stands in its path to

[1] Is. 2:1 ff.; Mi. 4:1 ff.

58

hinder. He is proclaiming that the main cause of the upheavals of human history is to be found neither in the moral defects (the feet of clay) that are bound to mark all human society, nor in the social and economic factors that can be analysed by skilful human research, but rather in the progress of the hidden kingdom of Christ which presses in on our present world from beyond, with powerful and even devastating effects on the things that happen around us. He is proclaiming for his own day the message of John the Baptist, 'Repent, for the kingdom of heaven is at hand.'[1] What Nebuchadnezzar had seen in his dream, and what Daniel was pointing to in his interpretation, was indeed the kingdom of God breaking into the midst of this world's affairs with irresistible and ever-growing power, smashing to nothingness everything that seeks to hinder its progress, and finally establishing itself, without rival and without opposing threat, as that which must stand and grow till 'every creature owns its sway'.

This is the Christ we have to proclaim today to this world of uneasy dreams, to its shaking and falling dynasties, to its crumbling empires, to its petty tyrants with feet of clay. In the New Testament Christ is himself described as 'a stone that will make men stumble' and 'a rock that will make them fall',[2] that brings doom to those who take no account of it and that shatters all Goliaths who defy the armies of the living God.[3] He is the precious cornerstone[4] which must define the shape of, and fill the supreme place within, all earthly empire-building; and woe to the foolish builders if they allow themselves to be tempted to reject him in order to fulfil other plans![5] To him, the man who has come into our midst in flesh and blood, and with his coming has brought in his kingdom in full reality, we must give all the significance that this flying stone gathers to itself in this great picture in the Old Testament. Here the significance of his incarnation, death, and resurrection and of his coming again are surely being pointed to.

What, then, does this colossal statue represent in our times? It can represent what is worst in the best of almost everything in the political and cultural world. It may, of course speak of something in the past. It can represent the Greek Empire, the Holy Roman Empire, Napoleon's empire, British imperialism, Hitler's empire. But it can also represent things in our more contemporary world. It can be a warning to American capitalism or Russian

[1] Mt. 3:2.   [2] 1 Pet. 2:6–8.   [3] 1 Sa. 17:41 ff.   [4] Is. 28:16.
[5] Ps. 118:22, 23.

communism. It can stand for any system that tends to close itself to the living influence of the Spirit of Jesus Christ. It can tell us all plainly what lies in our future too, if we dare to stand in the way of the progress of the Word of God by which he rules. His kingdom is bound to gather momentum and grow in hidden force and power. All that cannot be taken up and incorporated into it will ultimately be shown up as vanity—as chaff that the wind blows away. We need not give only a political significance to this colossal statue. It can stand for our little empires, domestic, social, business, financial or ecclesiastical in the midst of which some of us sit enthroned, trying in vain to find security and satisfaction. It can stand merely for the image of our own future.

But we shall never be at peace till we have really seen and acknowledged that this empire of ours, whatever it is, must give way before the coming of the kingdom of God.

The king's first response

The king, as he listened to Daniel, felt himself confronted with the reality of the truth. As he sat listening he knew himself there and then faced by the very kingdom that was being spoken about. As Daniel pointed upwards and into the future to the glory that was yet to be seen, Nebuchadnezzar was enabled to lift up his eyes. He, too, was given a vision and a foretaste of something more glorious, solid and lasting than the glory, might and business of the throne of Babylon which he had occupied so uneasily.

The chapter ends with a description of his *homage* done to Daniel (verse 46), of the tribute offered to the God of Daniel (verse 47), and of the appointment of Daniel and his three friends to exalted offices in the empire (verses 48f.). His response to the truth was not deep enough to change him radically, and we cannot call this an act of true repentance or a religious conversion, for in the next chapter we see him soon reverting to his paganism and his pride.

His behaviour helps us to realize that sometimes a religious experience can stimulate an impressive response at a superficial level and yet leave us untouched in the depths of our being. Nebuchadnezzar certainly uttered impressive words in favour of Daniel's God, but even in this panegyric he dragged him down to the level of one among other divine beings (verse 47). Certainly, too, he went through the emotional experience of a man who feels himself in the presence of Deity. Calvin's[1] comment is that in his confession of belief in the God of Israel, Nebuchadnezzar was seized merely by a 'violent' or 'sudden' impulse that constituted no true basis for repentance, and was 'not quite in his senses'. Yet Calvin conceded that considering the fierce pride of kings generally, it was remarkable to see him go thus far in giving this sign of piety and modesty. Calvin adds a note that even Pharaoh in the middle of his struggle against Moses was at one juncture so deeply impressed by what he saw of the 'power of the God of Israel' that he immediately gave glory to him.[2]

Yet Nebuchadnezzar made a good beginning towards true faith. In estimating the significance of the king's experience, we must note that at least on a psychological level it helped to bring a cure for his bad dreams. It did this by enabling him to begin to take his eyes off himself and off the petty affairs of his own kingdom. For it is because men have nothing 'high and lifted up' to raise their eyes to, nothing bigger than themselves and their own world to worship and wonder at, nothing more certain than their own ideas by which to steer their destiny, nothing more inspiring than their own goodness to lead them to repentance, that life grows stale, feverish and frustrated, and bad dreams become a matter of course. It would be good for some of us today if we could simply start where Nebuchadnezzar started that day—even though he did not then pursue the road to the end. New life and healing can come to us only when we begin to find purpose in pursuing not our self-centred aims but the glory of God himself, when we find rest in certainties that are completely beyond the changes and chances of human history, and find that we possess righteousness and peace only when we possess them as gifts from God himself. Nebuchadnezzar was brought for a moment to the threshold of this possibility, and it brought him at least a measure of satisfaction and relief.

[1] J. Calvin, *Commentary on Daniel, ad hoc.*   [2] Ex. 9:27; 10:16.

Daniel 3
The blazing furnace

The need for social cement

THROUGH his dream and its interpretation Nebuchadnezzar was brought for a moment to the threshold of great new possibilities for personal commitment. He received insights that could contribute to a new understanding of himself, and he was given at least a temporary cure for his bad dreams.

But he did not make the full commitment of his life to God that was now possible, and we are not therefore surprised to read the sequel in this present chapter. Nebuchadnezzar now reacts against the kingdom of God with the same degree of tension with which he previously felt drawn towards it. He used the help given to him by God in order to move himself further into independence of God. He soon allowed the system he had been living in to swallow him back, and we immediately find him perverting the very message through which God had tried to win him. He now easily excluded from his mind the more distant and unpleasant part of the message—the bit about the stone and its shattering impact on all earthly structures[1]—and he began to bathe in the encouragement the pleasant bit of the dream gave him, in its undoubted praise of the efforts he had been making.[2] That very word from Daniel's God, *you are the head of gold*, became to him a new charter to go on with his building!

But he did remember at least the one part of the vision that was immediately relevant to his task of building the great new society. That was the bit about the far-too-fragile feet on which the head of gold and the rest of the body were founded and the far-too-easily disintegrating mixture of part iron and part clay of which they were moulded. This part of the dream he took as a

[1]2:45.   [2]2:37, 38.

62

warning to himself about the lack of cohesion in the society he was re-structuring. The thought of it both unsettled him and spurred him on. He perhaps believed that he himself could see the tendency to disintegration, illustrated by the statue, working already around him in his empire of gold. He felt that he must ensure for his successors a better development. He must inject strong, enduring, and closely binding cement into his developing society.

What better and more lasting cement could there be than a common religion, and a culture deeply influenced by such a common religion? In these he believed he would find the nucleus around which a truly strong community consciousness could develop and grow. He would organize for its development.

It is no surprise then, after the dream, to find Nebuchadnezzar reasserting himself in a new burst of energetic social planning, carried out with fresh urgency, idealism and conviction. What he is now most concerned about is to exclude all possible sources of division and disintegration. Since he was an army man, we can even imagine him as desiring to create in civil life the same feeling of unity and community that he may well have experienced in his military campaigns! At any rate the individual must be made to feel that he belongs to something worth while, vital, and basically attractive. Nebuchadnezzar's aim is to develop and unify culture. But above all he requires a unifying religion, for religion itself was defined in parts of that ancient world as 'that which binds' and was acknowledged everywhere as the best kind of cement to keep a society together.

The Festival of the New Babylon

What came out of Nebuchadnezzar's renewed burst of social planning was the kind of thing that today would be called the 'Festival of the New Babylon'. It was proclaimed with much *éclat*. *Nebuchadnezzar made an image of gold, whose height was sixty cubits and its breadth six cubits* (verse 1). It was an unusually slim obelisk. It must have looked slightly grotesque with ninety feet of height and only nine of breadth, but it was possibly supported in its erect posture by a large base whose dimensions are not included in the specification given in the text. Certainly it was of immense cost if it was solid gold, and it must have made a startling impression even if it was simply gold plated. It was no doubt

63

meant to be hailed as a notable new feat of building technique and a new departure in creative design.

Commentators are divided as to whether the statue was meant to be the image of Nebuchadnezzar himself or of some Babylonian god. But in all likelihood the matter was left deliberately vague. The statue could represent whatever anyone wanted it to symbolize. It could stand for the spirit of Babylon, or for the emperor himself, or for one of the traditional national gods—or it could act as a syncretistic focal point for all the religions in his realm. Nebuchadnezzar knew that most would think of it as there to stimulate common devotion to the gods of Babylon whom he expected all people in some measure to serve. Yet he desired to leave minority communities within his conglomerate empire free to adapt the meaning of the outward ritual to their conscience about images and idolatry.

He did expect some measure of conformity. His programme would have been spoiled if any significant section began to talk of resistance or failed to join in. To help to win the enthusiasm of everyone, he laid great emphasis on the cultural aspect of the whole affair. The musical side was developed with special care. We can well imagine how Nebuchadnezzar set crash programmes in motion for teaching the various instruments (verse 5) that were to be most in use, got his composers busy and enlisted members to augment his orchestras. He may even have set about achieving a good blend of traditional folk music of every kind with new themes in a new idiom!

His programme was backed up by the kind of sanction which everyone expected in those days: a *burning fiery furnace* (verse 6) would be lit if necessary. Yet Nebuchadnezzar knew that no society could ultimately be held together by terror. The furnace was there only to deal with a possible lunatic fringe of anti-social cranks. The thought that sensible people could put themselves within reach of its flames hardly crossed his mind. He hoped it would not be needed in a programme open to such width of interpretation. Even those very religious people he had brought from the province of Judah, with their so-called 'supreme God' would surely not deny that the gods of Babylon had a right to be given prominence within the confines of their own territory. The festival was the thing—the solemn glorious inauguration of the cult—the music, the pilgrim excursions to the plain of Dura, the acts of devoted community celebration.

The miracle of resistance

It started off well. The first reports were exciting. Here, surely a fitting answer was being given by Nebuchadnezzar to the riddle and the question put to him by his dream: could there even arise a golden society, with feet, solid, broad-based and indestructible?

Then the report came through to the king that *'there are certain Jews whom you have appointed over the affairs of the province of Babylon: Shadrach, Meshach and Abednego. These men, O king, pay no heed to you; they do not serve your gods or worship the golden image which you have set up'* (verse 12).

The three who were seized upon may not have sought this open clash with Nebuchadnezzar's authority. They may well have tried quietly to avoid any too-open display of nonconformity. They may have hoped that no-one would take much notice of the fact that they were not often there when they knew the music was going to begin, and that when they found themselves involved, they quietly abstained from the more obsequious parts of the king's ritual. But they had thought through all the issues, made up their minds, and were well prepared in case it ever came to an open challenge. There was no hesitation in their answer when they were charged. They refused to give even one sign that there was any possibility of compromise or dialogue. *'Be it known to you, O king, that we will not serve your gods or worship the golden image'* (verse 18).

The answer

Their answer, under such a fierce and determined threat, took superb courage, and was given with extraordinary dignity. It illustrates again how faithful and loyal behaviour, sustained in a series of quiet decisions on less important matters, can come to glorious fruition in a spectacularly courageous witness to God in the hour of more severe and open trial.

They stress that they are not going to argue with the king. *'We have no need to answer you'* (verse 16). Indeed this reply is an assertion that it is now time to answer not in words, but in deeds. Nebuchadnezzar required to be taught that the God of Israel was not a mere talking point for religious discussion, but the living Lord of history. He required, above all, to know that the God of Daniel and of these three men could inspire not merely a king's dream but hard practical resistance, and undefeatable faith and courage. The king got their message more loudly and clearly as they stood before him silently resisting, and bravely facing the furnace, than if they had each preached a lengthy sermon. He knew already what they could hardly have put in better words. He had heard Daniel to his heart's content. He had had his remarkable dream. He knew enough of their law and tradition. At this moment what was most required was that the words that had been spoken almost too frequently and freely, really meant what they said.

There is 'a time to keep silence, and a time to speak'.[1] We need wisdom in order to know when to do which, and courage to neglect neither. Very often it is speaking time, and far too many of us shrink from proclamation and argument because we are ashamed, afraid, and unconvinced ourselves. But occasionally, as now with these men, speaking has to end and what we believe has to be demonstrated by action. Unless this silent sign in flesh and blood is given at the time it is called for, all our previous speaking is proved to be mere phoney chatter. Jesus gave himself to a ministry that consisted largely of speaking. But when he came to the time of his crucifixion he was more often silent. When he stood before his judges he forbore to speak at any length.[2] When he stood before Herod he lapsed into complete silence.[3] Few and brief were the words that came from the cross. His final answer was now to be given, like that of these three young men, in faithfulness and love and suffering. Yet the few sentences of witness to God that they do give by word of mouth are wonderful and deeply significant. They call him *our God* (verse 17). He is theirs, and they are his, for their hope that he will save them from the furnace is based on the deep covenant and personal relationship in which both as individuals and as members of the people of God they know themselves to live before him. He is *our God whom we serve.*[4]

Their confession of personal faith, coupled with the deep and close relationship that each has with God, moves on to reliance on his power to do whatever he has promised to do for them as their God. He *is able to deliver us* (verse 17). It has always been part of their creed from the beginning of their nation's life that nothing is impossible to God. He himself spoke such words to Sarah.[5] Moses lived by them and they were proved marvellously true at

[1]Ec. 3:7.   [2]Mk. 14:60 f.; Jn. 19:9 f.   [3]Lk. 23:9.
[4]*Cf.* Ex. 19:5; 20:2; Je. 31:33; Gn. 17:7.   [5]Gn. 18:14.

66

the Red Sea.[1] Jeremiah in their own day especially had made them his own and had found them true.[2] Now they are being re-echoed by the three witnesses before Nebuchadnezzar; and they are to come to life again in the teaching of Zechariah[3] and finally of Jesus[4] as he faces his own fiery trial in the garden of Gethsemane.[5]

So strong is their sense of being close to him, and their faith that their well-being is safe in God's hands, that they cannot imagine any ultimate harm at all coming to them from the hands of a petty pagan emperor. *'He will deliver us out of your hand, O king'* (verse 17). How can God possibly forsake those who are his? How can God's friendship now fail that has already proved as strong as the hands themselves? Yet at this moment they stressed their concern for the glory and vindication of God himself. They showed the same characteristic deference to the wisdom of God alone, as we saw illustrated in the previous chapter. They cannot themselves decide whether it is good for them to survive or perish. They believe he will answer their hope that they will come through alive; but *if not*, it is all the same, for the wisdom, glory and power in everything come from him.

The miracle of survival

Many of us will incline to accept the story of the preservation of these three men in the furnace as a faithful description of what happened there and then. If we believe in the living God of the Bible there is no reason why we should think it impossible that such an event took place. But there is no reason, especially at a point like this, for us to be unnecessarily offended or troubled if some find it difficult to read the narrative as a sober and exact account of how the sentence to death by fire was actually carried out by the king's executioners. We will miss the point if we stress too much the details of the miracle of survival. As Jacques Ellul points out in his discussion of the story of Jonah:

> The chief aim of the story is not to give historical information even though the miracle of the fish is quite acceptable, and I for my part see no objection to the possibility of a miracle of this kind. It is obvious that God's power can manifest itself thus. The main point to consider, however, is what the miracle signifies.[6]

[1]Ex. 14:21 ff.   [2]Je. 32:17, 27.   [3]Zc. 8:6.   [4]Mk. 9:23.
[5]Mk. 14:36.   [6]*The Judgment of Jonah* (Eerdmans, 1971), p. 45.

We must be careful not to become over-involved in what, for us reading the narrative, are secondary rather than primary matters: the chief point of the story is that in the fiery persecution that followed their brave act of witness, they came through completely unharmed. This chapter of Daniel repeats in the form of a historical narrative what a current hymn of the time said in song:

Fear not, for I have redeemed you;
    I have called you by name, you are mine.
When you pass through the waters I will be with you...
when you walk through fire you shall not be burned,
    and the flame shall not consume you.[1]

What struck Nebuchadnezzar as he watched them was: *'They are not hurt'* (verse 25). Their bearing and reaction could be put down only to some supernatural source of strength and comfort. The king knew that no matter what he did, nothing could in any way cut them off from this divine help. The more he persecuted them, the more he confirmed their witness. *'Did we not cast three men bound into the fire? ... But I see four men loose, walking in the midst of the fire ... and the appearance of the fourth is like a son of the gods'* (verses 24, 25).

The presence of the divine figure is no doubt meant to be taken as the fulfilment of God's promise of companionship with his people when they pass through tribulation. In many other stories in the Bible God gives signs of his presence in the form of the manifestation of an angelic being. It is naturally a Christian instinct to think of this also as a vision of the presence of the pre-incarnate Christ alongside those who are suffering for the sake of the kingdom of God. The writer of the letter to the Hebrews in his list of the great witnesses of Israel's past includes those who, by faith, 'quenched raging fire' as they, too, ran their race 'looking to Jesus'.[2]

It is remarkable too, that the fire of Nebuchadnezzar's wrath was also quenched by what he saw as he looked at these three men, and began to understand.

Nebuchadnezzar—the moment of truth

To return, however, to an earlier point in the narrative, the

[1]Is. 43:1, 2.   [2]Heb. 11:34; 12:2.

triumphant witness of Shadrach, Meshach and Abednego reminded Nebuchadnezzar with renewed force again about the dream which had earlier brought him so much agony—especially that bit about the stone which represented the kingdom-from-beyond which would not fit into the scheme of things laid down by man, even in his best and greatest efforts at empire building. Perhaps he now remembered vividly how time and again he had seen it and felt its penetrating and shattering power as it broke up and overthrew even the strongest earthly establishment that man could achieve. And here he was, being himself hit already by that very stone! Now he knew that in the resistance, dynamic power, and indestructible zeal of these three witnesses, in their calmness and peace as they showed their carelessness for all the rewards and threats of his own Babylon, he was experiencing this strange new kingdom which Daniel had preached to him from the dream. And now it was no longer a mere picture in a dream or words in a sermon, but was here before him as a political and personal force to be reckoned with in the affairs of his own realm. Perhaps, then, he began to ask himself deeply disturbing questions: Might not this painful confrontation be the beginning of the shock and clash that was ultimately to mean the break-up of all his fine schemes for universal and enduring rule? Might not the resistance of these three men be the pressure here and now of this everlasting kingdom, intimating to him that in sacrificing so much of himself for the new Babylon, he had made one of the worst mistakes of his life?

At any rate his reaction began with an outburst of wildly irrational rage. *Then Nebuchadnezzar was full of fury, and the expression of his face was changed* (verse 19). Was he being angry at what he had found out about himself in this moment of truth? Perhaps he knew now that his plans were not so perfect as he had thought, and that he had chosen too fragile a foundation for his building. He felt he had staked too much on his wrong choice. He had been a blind and careless fool to go on building his empire as he had, without remembering the kingdom of God.

When he gave vent to his anger, however, he directed it not at himself but at the three men before him: *full of fury . . . he ordered the furnace heated seven times more than it was wont to be heated,* and it was an order which, ironically enough, harmed his own executioners more than his intended victims (verse 22). This is not the first time that the Bible forces to our notice the fact that our inner hatred and anger (which can so easily reach the stage of 'fury') often finds as its victim not someone who is its legitimate object, but someone completely innocent of the harm against which we imagine ourselves taking vengeance. This is only one of several instances of how such irrationally misdirected anger can lead on to folly and tragedy. There is the story of Cain, angry with God and unleashing his hatred on Abel;[1] of the ten brothers venting their anger on Joseph without any just cause whatever for it;[2] and there is the story of Jonah angry at the plant when he should have been angry with himself for being angry.[3] And it all moves on (as so much of the Bible does) to what happened when Jesus came and there broke out on him the pressure of the whole great unrelieved mass of human frustration and hatred stored for centuries in the heart of a humanity whose deepest curse has ever been its own hatred of God and true goodness. There can be no cure for us until we recognize what our disease really is.

Nebuchadnezzar—the moment of repentance

As he passed through the moment of truth, Nebuchadnezzar passed through a moment of danger. He had suddenly to make the choice of allowing himself to become either humbled or offended by the truth as he faced it. In the end we know he allowed himself to be humbled. He ceased to resist the truth. He accepted the deadly wound it inflicted on his pride and self-confidence, and surrendered. His very fury turned out to be nothing more than the last defence of his pride before he gave in. But at the same time there was another way open to him. He could have allowed himself to become offended instead of humbled. He could have closed his mind, hardened his heart and confirmed himself in his proud resistance. The violence of his anger is proof of the intense and critical nature of the struggle he went through as he came to his decision.

His situation and his response can illustrate for us what Jesus meant when he said, 'Blessed is he who takes no offence at me.'[4] Jesus taught that wherever he was present, especially when he preached and healed, the kingdom of God was present 'in the midst',[5] and people were being challenged whether to enter it or reject it. Jesus knew that to those who were deeply committed to

[1]Gn. 4:8. [2]Gn. 37:19 ff. [3]Jon. 4:1, 9. [4]Mt. 11:6.
[5]Lk. 11:20; 17:21.

the structures, the wealth, the power and the lusts of this present world, the presence and challenge of the kingdom of God would call for radical change, and would be as deeply disturbing and as threatening as those three men were to Nebuchadnezzar, and as the stone in the latter's dream was to the earthly empires it ultimately broke up. Jesus therefore taught that those confronted with the presence of the kingdom through his own work and teaching would tend to take offence—to fight in anger against the truth that now confronted them and to become passionately resistant—as at first did Nebuchadnezzar. Blessed would they be if they could at this moment of offence begin to think again, relent, and change!

Nebuchadnezzar's final emotion as he changed his mind and allowed himself to be cut to the heart and brought to repentance was one of astonished fear. There is no doubt that what finally brought him to faith and commitment was the sight of the heavenly figure standing with and sustaining the very three he was persecuting. The New English Bible rightly describes him as *amazed and ... in great trepidation* (verse 24). On the day of Pentecost in New Testament times, three thousand people in Jerusalem reacted with the same repentant dismay when they realized, through the preaching of Peter, that God had raised up the Jesus whom they had hounded to death. They, too, had been wrong in their decisions about what mattered for life in this world. They too had made the mistake of their lives in rejecting him. They too were now faced with living undeniable proof of their wrongness and folly. The writer describes them as 'cut to the heart' in the process of coming to repentance.[1]

The king gave in and broke out into a doxology: '*Blessed be the God of Shadrach, Meshach, and Abednego, who has sent his angel and delivered his servants, who trusted in him*' (verse 28). Their survival meant his own personal deliverance too! And since he is an emperor, he accepts the practical political implications of his conversion and according to the light he has begins immediately to make amends. '*Therefore I make a decree: Any people, nation, or language that speaks anything against the God of Shadrach, Meschach, and Abednego shall be torn limb from limb, and their houses laid in ruins; for there is no other God who is able to deliver in this way.*' *Then the king promoted Shadrach, Meschach, and Abednego in the province of Babylon* (verses 29, 30).

[1]Acts 2:37.

Daniel 4
'I Nebuchadnezzar'

Evasion

IT becomes clear from even a superficial reading of this whole chapter that God had a demand to make of Nebuchadnezzar, a lesson to teach him and a question to ask him before his relationship with this man, begun so promisingly, could really become stable and fruitful. The demand was for the total commitment of his mind and heart and life to God himself. The lesson is three times clearly stated in the text (verses 17, 25, 32), *that the Most High rules the kingdom of men, and gives it to whom he will.* The question is obviously and simply that which he seeks to ask of all of us when he sees us living as if no-one in particular rules the kingdom of men: What is his aim and where does he think he himself is heading, with all this feverish and proud planning and building? It is exactly the question which Jesus in one of his parables imagined God to put to the rich fool—so like Nebuchadnezzar at this stage of his life—who had so much wealth that he tore down his barns and built greater ones, and became so impressed by the obvious greatness and security that all these gave him, that he said, 'Soul ... take your ease.'[1] God's question carried its own answer: 'Fool! This night your soul is required of you; and the things you have prepared, whose will they be?'[2]

This chapter is about how God pressed home his personal demand on Nebuchadnezzar in the later years of his life, taught him his final lesson and faced him with this ultimate question. It would seem that Nebuchadnezzar was consciously or unconsciously evading the demand, the lesson and the question. He seems to admit as much in his words: *'I, Nebuchadnezzar, was at*

[1]Lk. 12:19.   [2]Lk. 12:20.

ease in my house and prospering in my palace' (verse 4). This is meant to be read not simply as factual information but as an indication of exactly where the source of his trouble lay and a confession of where in his folly he went wrong. His prosperity was his danger and became his curse, his accepting of the delusive ease it was able to bring to him was his tragic undoing. Can we not imagine him looking over 'his great Babylon', which he had built, with an ever-growing inner conviction that this very achievement must have been the result of his faith in and indeed a reward for his service of the Most High God?[1] Surely such outward prosperity could be given only to one whose ways pleased this God in whose favour he had issued his great imperial decree! Was he not justified by the greatness of his very achievement with Babylon in taking some pride in himself as a religious man? It is true that in spite of all his progress in the way and worship of the Most High God something of the old paganism remained, pulling his life away from the truth.[2]

And, of course, in his very zeal for the task in hand, so full now of religious sanction, his mind became so prepossessed by false ambition and selfish concern that no room was left in it for true thoughts about God, and his time was so taken up that there was none left for listening to his voice. It thus became all the easier for him to evade God.

We can become so like Nebuchadnezzar—especially if our hard work has brought us some apparently solid achievement, and perhaps if somehow our careers have begun to be crowned with success. We, too, may have built something that looks impressive whether our line and our world be academic, commercial, professional or ecclesiastical. Surrounded by our achievements, especially if we are religiously inclined, we can begin to think such outward achievement must really have been the result and even the reward of some basic inner rightness in our life as a whole. Prosperity and success are always dangerous if they lead to 'ease'—and they are especially dangerous for those of us who believe in God. For the temptation always is to imagine that our very prosperity and success are signs that God is especially pleased with us and thus to delude ourselves into a false sense of happiness and security which diverts us from having to face the possibly unbearable truth about ourselves. Our life and effort, even our religious life and effort, thus become full of evasion.

[1] 3:28 ff.   [2] *Cf.* verse 8.

The rejection of the sower with the seed

Consultation is always the simplest and most reasonable way of settling a dispute—talking it over and facing it from every angle. And surely the deepest differences between God and ourselves can be best defined and faced and overcome by speaking to each other and treating each other as rational beings.

Therefore when he wants to teach us, convert us, and conscript us into his service God always first tries this—the most gentle way possible. He tries first of all to deal with us simply by telling us about his desires for us and about the kind of relationship he wants between us and him. He is a God who, to get his will or his way, uses words and prefers to use words. He prefers the way of drawing us out from within towards himself through our willing assent and co-operation rather than the way of moulding us to his own pattern by forcing it upon us from without. He prefers to plant a gentle seed in our hearts to create its own free response, rather than taking us in his hands for rougher treatment. He took this gentle way, for example, with Abram, when he called him out of Haran,[1] and he took this way with Moses when he sent him back to the desert to lead his people out of Egypt.[2] Even when he sent Isaiah to the sinful nation whom he knew might need some tough handling, his first appeal was, 'Come now, let us reason together.'[3] The same divine gentleness is found in the words 'I will be as the dew to Israel.'[4]

Nebuchadnezzar, then, must first be reasoned with. God wants him to listen and face his true situation within this relationship so that he can learn to avoid any possibility of a more harsh confrontation. But his mind is so much cluttered up day after day with his business that he has no time in his waking hours for serious thought or talk between God and himself. Therefore God gave him a dream. The Word came one night in an unforgettable way, and it got in where no word spoken directly otherwise would ever have got in, and the persistent and clear memory of it gradually forced itself on him till the dominant question day by day in his mind became: What can it all mean?

It was full of strange details. In it he saw himself represented as a great flourishing tree with abundant shelter for the multitude of *birds* and *beasts* which came around (verses 20–22). But at the height of its majesty and prosperity a *watcher, a holy one*, came

---

[1]Gn. 12:1 ff.   [2]Ex. 3:1 ff.   [3]Is. 1:18.   [4]Ho. 14:5.

down from heaven and ordered it to be hewn down. Its foliage was to be destroyed till only a desolate *stump* was left and the beasts and birds had to flee. This was to happen *till seven times pass over it*, presumably a period of seven years (verse 23). It was a warning to Nebuchadnezzar that he himself, great like that tree, but haughty and stubborn still in his pride, was going to undergo, if he did not change his ways and answer God's challenge and question, a tragic experience of being struck down with personal disaster—a period of prolonged insanity and isolation till he became truly humbled and renewed (verses 24-26). And the warning is blunt: *'Therefore, O king,'* said Daniel, *'let my counsel be acceptable to you: Break off your sins by practising righteousness, and your iniquities by showing mercy to the oppressed, that there may perhaps be a lengthening of your tranquillity'* (verse 27).

How gracious God was in trying to penetrate and influence this man's mind in such a frank yet gentle and subtle way—like the sower with the seed![1] And ample time was given for the seed to take root and grow till its inner influence was decisive. He was given a whole year to learn his lesson and change his attitude from the heart.

It was during this year that Nebuchadnezzar consciously said No! He either deliberately neglected or crushed out[2] the seed with the possibilities of its developing life. Moreover in this very response he was rejecting not only the message clearly put by Daniel, but also the way of simple and straightforward gentleness which God was so patiently seeking to take in his dealings with him.

The clay in the hand of the potter

Therefore God had to resort to a reserve plan and take a quite different way—and was he not provoked to doing it?

One day Nebuchadnezzar was walking on the roof of his royal palace, boasting audibly about the great Babylon he had built to the *glory* of his own *majesty* (verse 30), and a voice came from heaven: *'O King Nebuchadnezzar, to you it is spoken: The kingdom has departed from you'* (verse 31). The threat of the dream was fulfilled. With crushing force a load of relentless and most cruel suffering fell upon him. He was *driven from among*

[1] Mt. 13:3 ff.   [2] Mt. 13:7; *cf.* Dn. 4:20-22.

75

men, and ate grass like an ox, and his body was wet with the dew of heaven till his hair grew as long as eagles' feathers, and his nails were like birds' claws (verse 33). Whatever this means exactly, we are meant to understand that he underwent seven years in dreadful inward solitary confinement, that his whole personality seemed to be tragically deformed, in the severest kind of mental illness man can know.

As we compared God's former approach to Nebuchadnezzar to that of the sower with the seed, we can liken this new approach to the way of the potter with the clay. It was very similar to the way he had already taken in recent years with his people Israel, and the story of what Jeremiah had learned about God at the potter's house at Jerusalem was no doubt current among the people of Judah who were in Babylon. When everything was going wrong around him, and Jeremiah was in despair about anything ever going right again, he was told to go and look at the potter at work with his clay and his wheels.[1] The potter was at work on a piece of clay that would not yield to his plying and that developed faults as he worked with it. But the potter did not throw away his material. He started again with the same clay, with another plan and another touch, and he 'reworked it into another vessel, as it seemed good to the potter to do'.[2] The second plan certainly involved rougher and more prolonged treatment of the clay and it produced a new and perfect work.

As with the clay, so with Israel, and so with Nebuchadnezzar. God said through Jeremiah, 'O house of Israel, can I not do with you as this potter has done?'[3] Patient, gentle dealing had failed with Israel. Now there would come exile, ruin, and dreadful loss. Patient, gentle dealing had failed with Nebuchadnezzar. Now there had to come the seven years of mental anguish, till he learnt his lesson and was ready to make his commitment. God will never be thwarted by human resistance, nor will his wisdom ever fail to devise a new way, and his patience in the work will last long after we ourselves grow weary and despairing.

The Father who disciplines us

There is no doubt that today what is wrong with so many of us, whether we belong to the church or not, is that we will not listen to the word of God; we will not carefully face all the issues that

[1]Je. 18:1, 2.　　[2]Je. 18:4.　　[3]Je. 18:6.

76

require to be resolved between him and us, and we will not stop to ask with reason and good sense which way is the best and most blessed way to live. We seem, many of us, to have got beyond all such open, healthy discussion of issues, especially when it comes to our faith and our personal way of life. Perhaps we are now passing through the stage of the bad dream as Nebuchadnezzar did. Many people are thus uneasy about themselves, bewildered about the purpose and meaning of their lives and destiny, and are forced far too often to ask 'Who am I?' without knowing where to go with such a question. And not quite sure of anything, except that they are troubled, they will consult almost anyone who professes to be a 'counsellor'. It would be good if this deep disturbance in our dream consciousness could indeed lead many of us to listen again to the Word of God as it speaks in ways and words that are clear and understandable, and seeks to move us to a new life of commitment and obedience to God. But if we will not be reasonable, God will yet have his way. If we in the western world with all our Christian tradition, our still-functioning churches, and our learning and science, insist on going on to build our Babylon without the direction and inspiration of God, there may come, under the same hand and providence as once helped us to produce so many things worth living for, a time of much greater deprivation and darkness than we have known for centuries, till we learn again his ways. There may have to come to us the return to the dust and the clay before we are refashioned in the image of God—the dust and clay from which we were made in the beginning.

One further thought can give us some comfort if we ever find ourselves undergoing what we feel is strong-handed discipline from God. Let us remember that we are still in the same hands of the one who has always been patient and gentle. This was what Jeremiah further pleaded with Israel to realize. 'Behold, like the clay in the potter's hand, so are you in my hand, O house of Israel.'[1] It was the truth that Nebuchadnezzar laid hold of too. *'None can stay his hand'* (verse 35). The hands that crushed the clay were the same as had been stretched out previously in prolonged and gentle appeal. God did not change his nature when he took on the role of the potter, but remained the same in his purpose of love and grace. Therefore:

[1] Je. 18:6.

> My son, do not regard lightly the discipline of the Lord,
> nor lose courage when you are punished by him.
> For the Lord disciplines him whom he loves,
> and chastises every son whom he receives.[1]

When all this has been said from the story of Nebuchadnezzar, it remains for us to glance for a moment at a further light on the problem of suffering which comes to us from other parts of the Bible and especially from the New Testament. There is in the world, in greater measure than some of us realize, such a thing as purely innocent suffering. We ourselves, even, may feel that this story does not fully meet our own problem. We may feel that we have responded as fully as we can to the gentle ways of God and we are perplexed as to why things seem so hard and cruel for us. We have to remember the story of Job, the perfectly righteous man who suffered more than the unrighteous, and the story of the crucified one. Therefore we have at least two others to look at alongside Nebuchadnezzar.

Whatever happens to us, at least we can hold on to the fact that we are in God's hands. This is where basically we stand with Nebuchadnezzar and Job and Jesus. When Jesus was being crushed on the cross he had no doubt that he was in his Father's hands and he told his disciples so.[2] Moreover we have his word for it that we are always in his hands (and his Father's hands) and that nothing is able to pluck us out of his hands.[3]

How much it illumines our experience and our understanding of the meaning of all suffering to be able to listen to Jesus and look at Jesus even as we read about Nebuchadnezzar.

Daniel—companion and sign

Nebuchadnezzar came through his long period of trial and darkness. He learnt his lesson and became a new being.

In his testimony to his deliverance, he expresses gratitude for the one human being who had been able to help him. '*At last Daniel came in before me—he who was named Belteshazzar after the name of my God, and in whom is the spirit of the holy gods—and I told him my dream*' (verse 8). He acknowledges that Daniel had told him the truth clearly, before he himself had

[1]Heb. 12:5, 6; *cf.* Pr. 3:11, 12.　　[2]Jn. 16:32; Lk. 22:42; 23:46.
[3]Jn. 10:27-30.

78

grasped it and allowed it to reform his life.

So decisive is this praise of Daniel that it is reasonable to assume that he would be there years later to help the king as he came out of his time of insanity. There was some danger to Nebuchadnezzar in what he had to go through. He could have misunderstood it and become embittered. He could have failed to find his way triumphantly through the bewildering and devastating experience, and might have got lost within it. His great need, therefore, in facing what came to him and in interpreting it, was for someone to be with him, explaining its meaning, helping him to take the right attitude, and to come to the right decisions. He required a companion in conversation and prayer as he wrestled with the problem of his fearful suffering. God therefore gave him Daniel.

It is clear why he sought Daniel. He knew that only a man who had, as he phrased it, *the spirit of the holy gods* (verses 9, 18) could help him. He had found out for a second time how incapable were his magicians and enchanters, the *Chaldeans* and *astrologers* (verse 7), when it came to the kind of issue that was now before him. He must have a man who knew more and could speak about more than was contained in even the best counsel of the paid experts of his own great Babylon. So he turned at last again to the man who had once before spoken of things from beyond and had seemed to have a God who could be prayed to with some sense of reality.

Moreover the fact that Daniel was there with this man at this time is a reminder to us about our own need for each other at times when things, in a similar way, are hard for us, and difficult to understand. God does not always want us to work through our problems alone, and very often he does not leave us even to look very far for the help he means us to have. When he is working powerfully in our lives, and wants us to understand, he will often provide in friends—sometimes close to us in our family, sometimes in the pastor who preaches and visits—enough counsel and care to help us to come through our sorrows and difficulties and come out triumphantly. We should not be too proud or too nervous to seek and use such help. Often God wants to give it to us within the church community around us. What is important is that we try to find out what God himself has to say to us, and, for this, the expert who professes to give counsel on a purely secular level is not always the most helpful.

The presence of Daniel alongside Nebuchadnezzar can be quite significant for us. It can be to us a sign of the very presence of God there with the king in his suffering. When the king had to go through the hardest experience of his life God gave him a shepherd. When we think of Daniel as a representative of God it helps us understand what the psalmist meant when he spoke of the Lord as the 'shepherd' who is 'with me' as he went through the 'dark valley'.[1] We have to remember that even in the midst of all the afflictions which he himself sent to Israel in the exile he himself 'was afflicted, and the angel of his presence saved them'.[2] We have to remember, too, that as God gave Nebuchadnezzar a Daniel so he gives us, today, a Christ.

Daniel—faithfulness in counsel

When he faced the task of interpreting the king's dream, Daniel was *dismayed* (verse 19). Certainly he was honoured, but obviously from the start he feels helpless. His counselling is given with the same sense of his inadequacy for the task as Paul had. He offers his help with not the least trace of self-confidence, with no thought of playing the role of a trained expert, but in love mixed with 'weakness and ... much fear and trembling'.[3] Only God can make divine light shine into the life of this poor dark soul. Only God can plant the seed of new life in his heart, so empty and sterile. Only God can probe to the real cause of this man's illness, and only God can heal. It is sheer privilege to be called upon to act the part of a helper to another for whom God is seeking to do such things—to stand or sit alongside them—even to act the part of a midwife! But who of us with even the most expert training in the world can ever truly feel anything but helpless inadequacy when called to such a work?

Daniel's helplessness as he faced his task was mixed (like Paul's) with fear. He *was dismayed for a moment, and his thoughts alarmed him* (verse 19). He is reluctant and even shrinking! He knows well that what he will have to say to the king from such a text as this dream will be wounding and hard to receive, and he feels not a scrap of pleasure, for he loves the man he is confronting and he believes that God himself has no pleasure in such threatening. He hates the idea of involving anyone in such possible judgment as God's Word pronounces upon disobedience

[1] Ps. 23:4.   [2] Is. 63:9.   [3] Cor. 2:3; Eph. 4:2.

80

and failure to hear.

In his helplessness all he feels he can do is to look to God himself and point his fellow sufferer, too, away from his own trouble and weakness to God. Since it is God alone who can do what has to be done he does not obtrude his personality between the king and his dream. All he can do is simply to act as a waiting friend, helping the king to face with clearer honesty the Word of God that has been already spoken to him so directly from God himself. In his attempt to get Nebuchadnezzar to *lift* up his *eyes to heaven* (*cf.* verses 34ff.), the whole drift of what he says to him moves towards two statements: *'The Most High rules'* (verse 25), and *'Heaven rules'* (verse 26). It is a defect in so much of what today is called 'pastoral counselling' that it tends to focus the eyes of the patient on his own problems and inner state and far too little on God himself. But we will never be good Christian counsellors till we can somehow give people the help they need most urgently, the help to look away from themselves, their emotions and moods, their difficulties and mental problems, and 'fix both eyes' (as John Calvin emphasized so strongly)[1] on the mercy of God alone, and on his power too, as it is revealed in Christ. The problem of where ultimately we are going to direct people to look is of decisive importance in this matter of helping people in their troubles.

Yet in the midst of all his 'fear and trembling' over the stern aspect of the message, Daniel kept nothing back. Like Samuel when he received his message of doom for Eli and 'was afraid to tell the vision',[2] Daniel must have been severely tempted to hide something of the severest aspect of the word. In his sympathy he uttered his wish that the curse of the dream might have fallen on others and not on the king (verse 19). But he knew that only words of brutal frankness could have the strength to avert the coming calamity. There could be no cheap and immediate comfort for the man before him at this time, and no impression must be left on him that such was possible. Therefore the whole of the approach of Daniel and all his words must help to reflect to the king the critical position that he was in before God and the urgency with which he must face the message. The stern message had to involve the messenger too in its sternness.

In the midst of all hesitancy, moreover, Daniel forced himself to be quite specific and pointed in his message. *'It is you, O king'*

[1] *Institutes* 3.4.3. [2] 1 Sa. 3 : 15.

(verse 22), he says to him as he attacks him specifically for his pride. *'Therefore, O king'*, is his conclusion '*. . . break off your sins by practising righteousness . . . and mercy to the oppressed'* (verse 27). Nebuchadnezzar must not be allowed to interpret this dream as merely there to introduce him to some new, general truths about life, but as there to confront him personally with a particular and decisive challenge about the details of the way he had been living, the precise attitude of mind that he was adopting at that moment, and about what God wanted him to do there and then. A less courageous man than Daniel would have blunted the edge with which God was trying to pierce the heart in order to begin the healing process. The message could easily and comfortably have been dissolved into generalities that left a good momentary impression but in the end accomplished nothing definite.

'You are the man', said Nathan to David[1]—and only then did the eloquent and clever sermon begin to do its work. We tend to forget this when our task is to deliver the word. Those of us who are pastors, when we preach our sermons, slide far too often into an application of the Word so general and vague that no-one can possibly take offence and no life can possibly be changed. We tend to forget it also when we hear the Word. We too often hear (and read!) sermons from texts that taken fully and seriously should vitally affect our own way of living, but, alas, all that happens is that our mind becomes busy applying them to the world at large or to the other individual whom we name 'the man in the street'.

The lesson

What God wanted to say to Nebuchadnezzar above everything else is summed up and spelt out three times in the text of the chapter (verses 17, 25, 32), *that the Most High rules the kingdom of men, and gives it to whom he will.*

God rules! Nebuchadnezzar knew this. But where? Nebuchadnezzar answered: 'Up there!'

He was wrong, said Daniel—'Down here!' It was in *the kingdom of men* that he wanted his will done—in Babylon! He burned with zeal that men and women, nations and kings should wait on him to know what they should do, and that they should make his word and his will the basis of their political and social planning and of their personal lives. How close his word brings us

[1] 2 Sa. 12:7.

82

to the New Testament! In the same prayer in which we are taught to say 'Our Father who art in heaven', we are also taught to say, 'Thy will be done, On earth as it is in heaven'—for the Most High God cares about the way we deal with one another in our homes, about what we do with our bodies, and how we treat and provide for other people's bodies, about politics and sex and amusements and churches too—just as he cared about Babylon.

Moreover he *gives it to whom he will*. 'Who can inherit kingdoms?' thought Nebuchadnezzar before this sermon was preached to him. And of course he answered: 'The high born, the great, the powerful, the self-confident'—and he prayed for and sought this kind of kingdom.

But now he has come through his long agony and a much better kingdom than the one he sought and prized is really being given to him now—just as he is—to a poor, broken man, object only of the grace of God, and ready now to live by the grace of God. *'He gives it to whom he will, and sets over it the lowliest of men'* (verse 17). Now that he himself has been given this humility, has been brought to the point where he knows beyond all doubt that he has nothing to give, nothing to bring, and deserves nothing, he finds that he has received the kingdom. 'Blessed are the poor in spirit, for theirs is the kingdom of heaven ... Blessed are the meek, for they shall inherit the earth.'[1]

The personal testimony of a converted soul—his peace

The final section of this chapter reads like one of the psalms of thanksgiving for deliverance which are so frequent in the Bible. But the whole chapter is in the form of a letter. When we begin to read it we think we are in for a formal and paternal encyclical full of observations about the state of this world, about hopes for human society, welfare and brotherhood. *'King Nebuchadnezzar to all peoples, nations, and languages, that dwell in all the earth: Peace be multiplied to you!'* (verse 1). We have heard other sermons or addresses beginning like this and have immediately tended to go to sleep!

But what follows is not about the state of the world. It is, rather, about the state of his own soul. It is a truly personal story of his conversion—of a religious experience that opened his eyes, and changed his whole outlook and ways. It is about what God has

[1]Mt. 5:3, 5.

done to him as an individual. His ecumenical concern is simply that the whole world should know about himself, and through this testimony should know about God and come to know, each for himself, the peace the writer has himself received. *'Peace be multiplied to you!'* is for him now much more than a formal epistolary greeting. It means that he has had solved, as far as he himself is concerned, the question of his own lack of peace.

His evasion of God had been also an evasion of this question in particular. But now that he has faced it, he wants to help others to face it too—all this from one who has built so much, fought so much, possessed so much, and succeeded so well already! But he has never anywhere found anything so wonderful that he wants to write to the whole world in this way about it.

The personal testimony of a converted soul—his new-found life in God

Through being enabled to lift up his *eyes to heaven* (verse 34) his *reason* has *returned*. Twice this is mentioned (verses 34, 36), for this has been the physical and psychological miracle on which everything else has depended. It may be that a hint is here being given that we come to be truly in our right mind when we begin to view and value everything else in the light of heavenly realities.

The whole tenor of the psalm suggests that his life has received a new orientation, and that he has been thus delivered from aimlessness. *'My reason returned to me, and I blessed the Most High* (verse 34) ... *Now I, Nebuchadnezzar praise and extol and honour the King of heaven'* (verse 37). He has found something bigger than himself to live for—something bigger than even his mighty empire. He himself is so captivated and his energies and abilities and wealth are now so fully dedicated to this aim and end, that it is as if his whole purpose for life has been transformed.

He has been delivered, too, from isolation. He dwells on the transformation that he knows everyone around him has found in his own personality as a result of this new orientation towards God. *'My counsellors and my lords sought me, and I was established in my kingdom, and still more greatness was added to me'* (verse 36). Nearly every other glimpse we have of this man is of one living in tragic isolation with people around him only because he had power to compel and rewards to give. But now something has happened that people can sense and see, and the barriers of isolation in his own being are broken through and people seek him, as he seeks them. He has become open to fellowship and knows himself called to it.

He ends the psalm with a testimony to his deliverance from *pride* (verse 37). This sin has blighted everything he has done, separated him from God, made him hard to live with, and has made him preoccupied with only his own glory. The beginning of the psalm is closely connected with the end. It was what he saw when he lifted up his *eyes to heaven* (verse 34) that brought him in to such deep self-abasement. Massillon's great funeral sermon for Louis XIV, preached in Notre-Dame and no doubt preached in full view of the open coffin of the dead king, began with the twice repeated cry, 'Only God is great!' Nebuchadnezzar had discovered this, and thus the starting-point for a life of humility. *His dominion is an everlasting dominion, and his kingdom endures from generation to generation* (verse 34).

Jesus called what Nebuchadnezzar had found 'life'. He was referring precisely to the question which Nebuchadnezzar had faced here, when he spoke about how people could lose, or find, and thus gain their lives.[1] And he urged the importance of the issues we have read about in this personal testimony when he said, 'What does it profit a man, to gain the whole world and forfeit his life?'[2] Nebuchadnezzar on the way to gaining the whole world has been saved from personal disaster. For us to gain the world and forfeit our life can be only too easy. It can mean allowing ourselves to become completely absorbed in solving every other question around us except this ultimate and too often neglected one.

As if to underline the importance of the personal issues raised in this chapter, the same theme is taken up again in the next chapter, and is there pressed home with even greater force as a matter of life or death. Indeed the whole aim of this central section of the book of Daniel is to raise this issue of personal salvation. In this chapter one king is saved because he faces it squarely and answers with repentance and faith. In the next chapter his successor is condemned because he refuses to do so. In spite of all the urgency of community or state business, even the king cannot escape this challenge.

[1]Mt. 10:39; Lk. 14:26; Jn. 12:25 f.   [2]Mk. 8:36.

Daniel 5
Belshazzar's feast

Nebuchadnezzar and Belshazzar—the drawing of a contrast

AT this stage, it is worth pausing to note certain critical problems which we are bound to consider if we are concerned about the historical accuracy of the text of Daniel, and whether it was written in the sixth century or at some other time. It should be noted that though these questions have some importance, they do not radically affect the actual message of the book as much as many people imagine. On reading the fifth chapter, the ordinary 'lay' reader of the book will receive the impression that the new *'King' Belshazzar* (verse 1) was actually the son of Nebuchadnezzar, and succeeded him on his death. When Daniel addresses him he refers to Nebuchadnezzar as *'your father'* (verse 11). The text also suggests that at the end of the incident in which *Belshazzar was slain* there was a military coup by the army of the Median emperor Darius who took over power in the city (verses 30, 31).

Yet all the results of historical research so far tell us that Nebuchadnezzar was not actually succeeded by any blood relation but by a usurper named Nabonidus, that the son of Nabonidus, Belshazzar, was never king of Babylon, that no-one called 'Darius the Mede' can be traced in historical records, and that Babylon fell to Cyrus the Persian. One account tells us that there was no struggle when Babylon fell, and that the people gave Cyrus a hero's welcome. Another account says that the invaders entered the city by stealth and that Cyrus, along with his officers, took the royal palace by surprise and killed the king after only some slight resistance.

Faced by such evidence, the historicity of Daniel can be defended along a number of lines. For example the word 'father' could be used in the unspecific sense of 'predecessor'. It is also suggested that the real father of Belshazzar, Nabonidus, was ill on leave of absence, and had probably appointed Belshazzar as regent when Babylon fell. Therefore in this sense he was recognized as 'king'. It can be held that 'Darius the Mede' was another name for an officer of the Persian King Cyrus, called Gobyras, whom Cyrus appointed to rule Babylon for an interim period after his conquest of the province. Some have tried to solve the problem of 'Darius the Mede' by suggesting that he was really Cambyses, the son of Cyrus, or Astyages, the last Median emperor who was at this time a prisoner of Cyrus, and who could have been released and given the throne of Babylon for a short period.

But what is most likely is that the writer of the book of Daniel was chiefly concerned at this part of the book not to relate a consecutive story but to select from the facts he knew in such a way as to get across the message to be found in the striking contrasts which stand out when two men, so close to one another historically, receive the Word of God and respond to it.

If we become too concerned with the issues raised by the historical problems we may fail to notice the striking contrast which the book at this point seems designed to convey—the contrast between God's final word to Nebuchadnezzar and his final word to Belshazzar. With deliberate intention the traditional story about Belshazzar, his vision, his judgment and his bad end, has been placed next to the corresponding story of Nebuchad-nezzar, his dream, his judgment, and his good end. The purpose of this arrangement is to bring home to us that even in the 'heathen' world outside the sphere of Israel's inner life, while some men seem to be elected by God, others, alongside, seem at the same time to be rejected. The intention is to illustrate in the most vivid way possible that the Word which gives life to one can also bring death to another, and that the form of the Word of God in each case is different.

Nebuchadnezzar and Belshazzar and Daniel—even 'change' can change!

The most obvious lesson brought out as he underlines the contrast between these two rulers is how swift a deterioration can take place in the wake of even good and sound community reformation. Certainly Nebuchadnezzar's conversion did bring about 'change' in Babylon, both in ethics and outlook. There is no reason to doubt that it led to his practising righteousness and showing mercy to the oppressed.[1]

It is indicated that towards the end of his days, as he put his enlightened policies into force, many of his *counsellors* and *lords* were deeply impressed,[2] and no doubt after his death they sought to follow his example. But evidently the vision was lost, the force of the movement petered out, the originally inspired word lost its life in merely imitative repetition. The story of the conversion of the emperor which had once hit the headlines became a vague historical memory with no apparent relevance.[3]

We are meant to note one central and decisive point of difference as we move from the account of the reign of Nebuchadnezzar to that of his successor. We saw Nebuchadnezzar treating the sacred vessels of the God of Israel with respect and decency.[4] We now see Belshazzar using them sacrilegiously only to add a little novelty to his last drunken orgy (verse 3). This kind of action, and any common consent to it, would have been even unthinkable in the earlier reign. The change in attitude has been radical and it has come about with remarkable speed (for only a few years separate Nebuchadnezzar's last dream from this final affair), and by reading between the lines we can note other significant trends in the change in life-style and cultural outlook. Nebuchadnezzar had a zeal for education that we find difficult to attribute to his successor. Indeed permissiveness seems to have replaced discipline—and we can imagine that few of the counsellors and lords who were attracted to Nebuchadnezzar as he put through his final reformation would be among the courtesans and rakes who *praised the gods of gold and silver, bronze, iron, wood, and stone* (verse 4) as they drank themselves drunk at Belshazzar's feast.

The men who brought about this further transformation of life in Babylon, Belshazzar and his like, were not determined fanatics launching a planned anti-God campaign. They simply let things slide, and very casually put Daniel on the shelf. They did not even respect him enough to bother persecuting him.

Daniel's attitude

Daniel's attitude is remarkable. He must have had cause for deep

[1] 4:27.   [2] 4:36.   [3] 5:18–23, esp. 22.   [4] 1:2.

concern. He must have expected that the work God had so certainly begun in the previous generation would prove more obviously lasting in its influence. No doubt the disappointment taught him the healthy lesson of avoiding quick mass media assessments of moral or spiritual change. But obviously the experience did not make him cynical or pessimistic or withdrawn. He prospered during the next reign. He held himself available all the time, and he was back at his desk and his job as soon as he was recalled—still trying to change things for the better.

We, too, can learn from the Bible here to be both optimistic and sober in the expectations we give ourselves about social, political, and even church reform. We need never be cynical about trying to transform people and situations. God is the God who does work change. The Bible and all Christian experience bear witness to many reformations that have taken place in individual lives and even sometimes in social structures—changes that have endured all the attacks of time and every test of history. But sometimes change, even under God's very direct agency, does not fulfil its promise. This is true especially of these quick transformations that sometimes come about in the 'morale' of communities, and it can even be true about structural changes in any society. The situation brought about by a revolution can often, after the first flush of success, descend to a lower level than before the change and stagnate there. It all depends on whether the vision under which the change was brought about can be maintained, and if the force of the Word that inspired it remains fresh and powerful, and if the people involved continue to fight for the sake of even better change.

Therefore we must not trust in change, but only in the God who brings it about, and in the Word which commands it. We must never rest content with a measure of change, but always seek to bring what has been achieved under the fresh criticism, power and inspiration of the Word of God. We must be careful never to build our hopes too much on the successes we have had already.

Jesus said many encouraging things about our being 'salt' and 'light' and 'leaven'[1] and thus being able to wield a strong influence in the place where we have room and contact; nevertheless he warned us that as history progressed evil would develop along with the good,[2] and he painted rather a lurid picture of the kind of

[1]*Cf.* Mt. 5:13-16; 13:33.   [2]*Cf.* Mt. 13:30.

government we might find ourselves under as time goes on.[1] The teaching of the rest of the New Testament, too, is just as sobering as that of the book of Daniel. Emperors can be very good and helpful,[2] but then the anti-Christian spirit lurking around, and even within, the church can easily introduce the era of persecution which Christians must patiently watch for too.[3] We must always be prepared for the fact that people around us, as God warned Ezekiel, may 'hear or refuse to hear'.[4] Whatever the sphere in which our task lies—in government, parish or family – sometimes what we say and do will be really welcomed, really listened to, really accepted. But sometimes we will find ourselves completely 'out of season',[5] and this may mean the accusation that our day is completely over. Nevertheless we are to work with the same urgency and zeal, whatever the visible response, wait and watch and pray with the same hope. Daniel learned such waiting, and the time came when he was really wanted and listened to once more. Things around us can move as swiftly one way as another.

Nebuchadnezzar and Belshazzar—the elect and the rejected

The two men we have been discussing stand within the context of a long series of contrasting figures within the Bible.

Holy Scripture often lights up for us the extraordinary nature of the effect of God's grace on some of its great elect figures by contrasting them with others, who seem by reason of the very contrast to have a shadow of rejection cast over them. Along with Abel, for example, we have Cain who hated God and committed murder. Along with Jacob, who after his long struggles ultimately surrendered to God, we have Esau. Along with David there is Saul. Alongside the eleven faithful disciples there is Judas. And so we have Nebuchadnezzar and Belshazzar.

What is it that ultimately and basically determines the difference between two such men as Nebuchadnezzar and Belshazzar, as Jacob and Esau; between the one to whom God is predominantly the merciful friend who saves, and the other to whom God appears predominantly as the inexorable judge who condemns? Holy Scripture puts the whole difference down to the sheer sovereignty, wisdom and grace of God.

It is always a mystery why one should seem to be elect, another

[1]*Cf.* Lk. 21:12 ff.   [2]Rom. 13:1 ff.   [3]Rev. 13; 17:10 ff.
[4]Ezk. 2:5.   [5]2 Tim. 4:2.

seem to be rejected. One aspect of the mystery is the unsearchable decision of God. 'Jacob have I loved and Esau have I hated.' 'He has mercy on whoever he wills, and he hardens the heart of whomever he wills.'[1] As we go back to the biblical narrative, and read again the stories of these contrasting characters, we are bound to admit this side of the mystery. God does seem to choose and reject, to raise up and to cut down. We are not being faithful to Holy Scripture if we fail to make this emphasis.

But as we read the stories, we cannot fail further to notice that it was also through the personal and real decisions of each man before the gracious God that his purposes were worked out: the absolute justice of the workings of sovereign grace is displayed by allowing us to see that each received what his response merited. Human decision is thus seen as a factor, even if secondary, helping to determine which aspect of God's twofold work was to have pre-eminence within the divine-human relationship.

There seems no doubt that the approach of God to each of these two, the elect and the rejected, was the same from the start. It is not his will that any should perish.[2] He always prefers his merciful work to his judgmental work. Mercy is appropriate to him. He delights in it. Judgment is strange to him[3]—it is his shadow-side, and he wants it always to remain so. Therefore he comes first and always to men and women in mercy, and we have seen how Nebuchadnezzar opened his life and found he was indeed opening it for the merciful response of God.

The rejected chooses his rejection

What about Belshazzar? The very fact that he is set so closely alongside Nebuchadnezzar, so that point-to-point comparison can be made, allows us to assert that he was in a position to have exactly the same grace shown to him—though perhaps in a different form. An indication is given to us that he *knew* (verse 22) about Nebuchadnezzar's remarkable experience and testimony. It is a fair assumption that when he started his reign he could have seen enough and heard enough, had he desired to see and hear it, to have convinced him of the genuineness of the motives of his predecessor. But he refused to respond in any way to this surrounding grace. The word was allowed no inner place in

[1]Mal. 1:2, 3; Ex. 33:19; 4:21; Rom. 9:13, 18.   [2]Ezk. 18:23, 32.
[3]Mi. 7:18; Is. 28:21.

which to work—no root-hold. Therefore by the grace of God the absurd had to happen. The shadow-side, or underside, of God's work and activity appeared to take prominence. Belshazzar, in the decision of his free will, found himself met by a God determined to take his 'strange' way with him, wilfully committing himself to look into the face of wrath and not that of grace.

He who was rejected is held responsible for choosing to be so. There was that in each that clearly justified what happened. Holy Scripture, however, does not attempt to give any reasons for the salvation of the elect. Nor does it attempt to bring everything in the problem clearly together to show how the mystery of the choice of man logically, or even justly, fits into the mystery of the decision of God. The realities of life and of the faith, as they come out in this matter, do not fit into our human logic.

What comes out clearly within this dynamic encounter is that when Belshazzar so perversely said No! to God, his refusal served only to demonstrate, justify and seal upon his experience the fact that God was saying No! to him. And God was saying No! with the same almighty power and unquenchable zeal as was behind his desire to save this lost man. God is always Lord, even when a man is being perverse, and being damned because he refuses to be saved. This means that Belshazzar was rejected while Nebuchadnezzar was elected. Yet he who was rejected deliberately chose to be so, and he who was elected deliberately responded to the grace that saved him.

Nebuchadnezzar—mercy and judgment

No encounter that we ever have with God can from our point of view be one-sided. No matter what God says and does when he speaks with men and women, whether he saves or condemns them in his word and action, there always seems to come before us two sides of his activity and his being—one revealing mercy and the other revealing righteousness. In the mercy we encounter the righteous judgment. We are not 'accepted' by God without at the same time being judged and condemned by the God who is justifying us. We are never made whole by him without at the same time being broken by him, for when we are 'made new' the old things have to be made to 'pass away'.[1] Yet even when our experience of God is dominated, as sometimes happens, by the

[1] *Cf.* 2 Cor. 5:17.

92

fearful and shattering judgment of God, we can never fail somehow to encounter the merciful aspect of God even in our experience of judgment.

The narrative of the book of Daniel so far has shown us in the case of Nebuchadnezzar how mercy acts alongside judgment. In and through all the experiences that came to him under the pressure of God's grace there is not the least doubt from beginning to end that this man is being as gradually and gently as possible won for the service of God. The word is even breathed, as it were, from within his mind into his dreams. Even as we watch him undergoing the harsh shock treatment at the end of his days there is no alteration in the fact that God is working all things together for a positive purpose. He does not fail to play the part of one who cares and is there to woo this man to himself in friendship. Mercy is in the foreground, judgment is in the background.

Belshazzar—judgment and mercy

But as we move from Nebuchadnezzar to Belshazzar in his last days, the whole approach of God seems on the surface to be completely different. Judgment is in the foreground, and mercy remains in the background. This is not an affair of friendship, but of cold, unwavering, carefully calculated judgment. The atmosphere is that of the courtroom—or, rather, of the executioner's antechamber. Now the word of God does not come as it did to Nebuchadnezzar, wrapped up tantalizingly but familiarly in his own dream imagery, but is thrust on him in harsh confrontation in the writing on the wall—in a form alien and threatening and starkly objective—over against him. It came with such menacing strangeness that his reaction could only be awe and terror. The contrast is so striking that it almost seems to be a 'different God.'

That is what took place as it appeared on the surface that last day of Belshazzar's life. We know that it was not a 'different God,' that in the midst of such a final judgment there was at least one sign of mercy, for Daniel was there to help him to repent if he cared. We can confidently assert that the affair of the writing on the wall was only the climax of a long process in which this man had come to know exactly what he was rejecting when he refused to follow the way of Nebuchadnezzar. It was the same God who showed such judgment to Belshazzar as showed mercy to

Nebuchadnezzar. Such was the way with one man. Such was the way with the other; and both ways reveal true and worthy aspects of the one loving and gracious God.

When Paul wrote giving examples of the 'kindness and the severity of God', he added a warning: 'Do not become proud, but stand in awe.'[1] When the Bible brings before us so clearly and pointedly stories of degradation, tragedy and disaster such as we have in Belshazzar, alongside stories such as that of Nebuchadnezzar, we must not imagine that only the latter has relevance and that there could be no possibility of our travelling the way of Belshazzar. This man too is here so that we can learn from him. His story stands out like a sign on the top of a dangerous rock, warning us to keep away and directing us to the safe navigation channel. It warns us that we can all drift easily into the habit of trifling with God, that can gradually lead on through continued neglect and a quiet and steady hardening of mind and attitude to deeper and more serious forms of resistance, till we cease to care about what once would have moved us, and cease to be ashamed or blush[2] at what once would have shocked us. We can too soon arrive at this point of disaster unless we know our weakness and guard against it. It is for this reason that the Belshazzar story is there for us—not simply to be read with interest as a vivid but, for us, irrelevant description of the way of the wicked, but to stand as a warning to those of us who believe ourselves still in grace. It is for us to 'see to it' that we do not 'fail to obtain the grace of God'.[3]

The writing on the wall

They drank wine, and praised the gods of gold and silver, bronze, iron, wood, and stone.

Immediately the fingers of a man's hand appeared and wrote on the plaster of the wall of the king's palace, opposite the lampstand; and the king saw the hand as it wrote. Then the king's colour changed, and his thoughts alarmed him; his limbs gave way, and his knees knocked together (verses 4–6).

It is an unforgettable picture. The atmosphere of the day of final doom prevails as soon as the hand starts writing. It is because he senses this that Belshazzar's whole physical being is so badly

[1] Rom. 11 : 20—22. [2] *Cf.* Je. 6 : 15. [3] Heb. 12 : 15.

convulsed. Daniel spells out the impending disaster as he reads and translates: *MENE, MENE, TEKEL, and PARSIN* (verse 25).

The three words used here are interpreted by some to represent three weights in a descending scale — 'a hundredweight, a pound and an ounce', or 'a dollar, a dime and a cent'. The simple reading of these words in one of these ways would have been enough to warn the king that he was indeed on the path of degeneration and had lowered the entire status and worth of his kingdom to the point of its rejection by God.

Having read the words superficially, Daniel then went on to take a further mysterious meaning by using the consonants making up each word and going back to their original root meanings. He therefore derived a further threefold meaning for Belshazzar:

MENE = numbered, and ready for sale
TEKEL = weighed, and found wanting in substance
PARSIN = divided, *i.e.* given over to the Medes and the Persians

The act of sacrilege

It is a striking fact that in Daniel's sermon the one particular sin for which Belshazzar is condemned is not his intemperance or his free indulgence in the sensual, but simply his deliberate act of sacrilege. Yet we may be puzzled as to why such an apparently trivial action brought such severity of judgment upon itself. Why should God make such a fuss about the use of a set of golden cups from a temple he seemed to have deserted—belonging to an era now well in the past? Moreover, it could be argued that no human being was directly harmed by what was done. No cruelty was involved—no inhumanity of man to man.

What special significance, then, had these sacred vessels, so that their abuse was regarded as so serious a sin? The tradition of Israel taught that God chose certain people and certain things for his own special use. Simply because of his choice, and not because of any inherent quality they possessed in themselves, these people or things were to be regarded as 'holy' and were called 'holy.' For instance, the people of Israel as a nation are called in the Bible the 'holy' people, because God called them in this way.[1] The temple is

[1] *E.g.* Dt. 7:6–8.

called the 'holy place', because God chose it as his dwelling place where he would meet with his people.[1] Moreover, God established a cult with an elaborate ritual for this temple. He had things and people set apart specially from the common uses they were put to in the world around, and consecrated for his own exclusive use as he drew near in the worship of the temple. These people and things—the priesthood, the vestments, the altar, the vessels used on it, the candlesticks too, were in the same way regarded as having a special holiness simply because God had chosen them, had called for them to be set apart, and accepted them for this kind of service.[2] When the temple was built and ready with all its paraphernalia to be dedicated to him, he himself came in a cloud and filled the whole place with his 'glory', as if he had accepted all these things for his service for ever.[3]

Another way of expressing the fact that the temple altar and vessels had a peculiar sanctity was to say that God had put his 'name' upon them,[4] so that when they were used in the cultic worship, and his 'name' was called upon in prayer and worship, he would honour and bless the holy use to which they were put.

The vessels which Belshazzar abused were those which had been set apart for God's exclusive use, those to which he had connected the use of his name in such a gracious way. To treat such vessels with contempt was a defiance of the third commandment: 'You shall not take the name of the Lord your God in vain; for the Lord will not hold him guiltless who takes his name in vain.'[5] This commandment is not simply a prohibition of swearing or perjury. It is a prohibition of any kind of perverted or vain use of that which God has given us for the purpose of seeking his presence and calling on his name in prayer and worship.

Moreover, when Belshazzar paraded the vessels before his table and made their abuse the highlight of his drunken orgy, there was defiance and presumption in his action. It was a sign indeed that he believed that this God, whose vessels he was abusing and whose name he was insulting, had now in Babylon no reality or power. Belshazzar had counted him out. Therefore in the action there was a challenge to the God of Israel. Belshazzar despised holy things because he despised God—and he crashed himself against the rock of Israel's God. He must now learn that he was the living God, always watchful over his own concerns as

[1]*Cf.* Ex. 29:43–46; 1 Ki. 8:10; 9:3.   [2]*E.g.* Ex. 40:9–11.
[3]*Cf.* Ex. 40:34, 35; 1 Ki. 8:10, 11.   [4]*Cf.* Dt. 12:11.   [5]Ex. 20:7.

well as those of his people and of humanity, never lightly discarding what he had called to belong to himself, and had therefore endowed with sanctity and set apart for his special use in drawing near to men and women.

The vessels of the Lord

In every age men and women are put to the same test. God still has his holy vessels today and we too are often being tested as to our use or abuse, our care or neglect of them. We often call them today the 'means of grace' to which God finally and decisively attached his name when in Jesus Christ he came and lived and died and rose again. These 'means of grace' are the Word and sacraments (baptism and the Lord's supper). These are given to us by God as signs to which he has chosen to attach his presence and his power within our worship. The danger for most of us today is not so much that of committing Belshazzar's kind of sacrilege. Such coarse behaviour is today usually punished by law as a criminal offence. Our temptation is simply to the careless use and light-hearted neglect of these means of God's grace. We treat the church, its services and sacramental worship, as if it had no greater significance than the coffee house or the public bar—and we sometimes talk as if they had lost their significance even for God himself.

In the New Testament, the members of the church are warned in the severest terms against this subtle kind of sacrilege,[1] especially against carelessness in the use of the Lord's supper,[2] against a casual approach to the life and worship of the community.[3] We must not too readily imagine that because we ourselves are keen on progress and change, this necessarily means that God has lost his concern and care for things that he has named as his own and appointed as means of his grace. It is certainly true that God himself is free to clear his cupboards, as it were, to throw off as outdated whatever he has honoured and used in the past. But we ourselves are never free either to discard, like Nebuchadnezzar, or to abuse, like Belshazzar, what God has sanctified by his own choice and usage. And on our own initiative we must never assume that he has done so.

We can think of even wider applications of the term 'vessels of the Lord'. Around the sphere of the church's life there are a whole

[1]Mt. 21:13.   [2]1 Cor. 11:27 ff.   [3]1 Cor. 11:17 ff.; 10:21; Acts 5:1 ff.

range of vessels that are more sacred to him than we sometimes imagine. A recent commentator likens the set of vessels which Belshazzar desecrated to the set of conceptual language forms and mental imagery which God used in the Bible, and has used in the church too, down the centuries. Such an application can be of special significance to all of us who work often and closely with Holy Scripture, as we discuss and shape our theology and ethics, and as we teach and preach. In all such processes the Bible, on being used, has to be analysed and studied scientifically. In this process we look at it from all the points of view that we use when we examine any other book. Yet in the midst of this activity the way we handle Holy Scripture can become a true reflection of our own deep inner attitude to God. Even using the best scholarship in the world, we are challenged as to whether we at the same time accord it unique reverence as indeed something 'holy', or profane it. We have to remember, too, that not only the words but also the ways of thinking and the imagery given to us through the book have their own sanctity and therefore may have a unique validity for us in every age. The passing of time does not tempt God to forget and discard the old, as we with our feverish yearning for change often imagine.

We must not forget, either, that God lends his own image to all men and women, and that the abuse of human personality and freedom can become as sacreligious an act as that which brought Belshazzar to his doom. Nor must we forget that as we belong to him our bodies are 'the members of Christ', the 'temple of the Holy Spirit' within us.[1]

The essence of sin

Belshazzar's behaviour, and Daniel's interpretation of it, helps us to understand the biblical teaching about what 'sin' really is in its essential nature. Daniel emphasizes that Belshazzar knew fully the implications of what he was doing—'*You knew all this, but you have lifted up yourself against the Lord of heaven*' (verses 22, 23). His sin was an absurd and deliberate choice of darkness over against the full shining of the light.

In the New Testament the apostle Paul defines this essential character of sin as being 'hostile to God',[2] and he points out that in this hostility man deliberately perverts what truth of God is

[1] 1 Cor. 6:15, 19.   [2] Rom. 8:7.

98

known to him and turns it into a lie.[1] The apostle John defines it as 'lawlessness',[2] and a love of darkness rather than light.[3] Here already in the book of Daniel we find that what makes a sin really sin is the decision of the will, in the full light of knowledge, not to receive the grace of God, or to acknowledge his light, or to keep his law, but in hatred of him to prefer darkness and lawlessness. In such an attitude and decision of will against the living God there is always the element of the irrational, demonic and absurd (a point which we will take up again in our next study).

When Jesus was on his way to the cross, he expressed clearly in some of his sayings his own deep feelings about what the people around him were doing to him. What appalled him in their attitude to him was precisely what appalled Daniel in Belshazzar's attitude to God. It was their absurd and deliberate choice of darkness in face of the full shining of the light, their absurd and deliberate choice of chaos instead of order, of death instead of life. In his warnings he stressed their deliberate exercise of an evil will. 'You refuse to come to me.'[4] 'How often would I have gathered you . . . and you would not!'[5] In the climax of his parable of the wicked husbandman he showed the men of power in Jerusalem that their absurd and perverse decision to reject and kill him was being made with clear knowledge of what they were doing. 'Afterward he sent his son to them, saying, "They will respect my son." But when the tenants saw the son, they said to themselves, 'This is the heir; come, let us kill him and have his inheritance.'[6]

The pastoral word at the eleventh hour

Daniel was there for Belshazzar as he had been there for Nebuchadnezzar. He was there waiting to be called in, and ready to speak. He was there in the place of God himself, and with the help of God for this pitiful man before him. Was this not a sign that God was waiting even for an eleventh-hour repentance from this man, even in face of the brutally final challenge of the writing on the wall? Expositors sometimes take this line, giving illustrations of how in the Bible other men have come to God in repentance at the last moment. If such a turn had taken place (and who can say that it could not have taken place?), Daniel could have

[1]Rom. 1:18–25.   [2]1 Jn. 3:4.   [3]Jn. 3:19.   [4]Jn. 5:40.   [5]Mt. 23:37.
[6]Mt. 21:37, 38.

spoken the same kind of pastoral saving word as he had spoken years ago to Nebuchadnezzar.

But such a word did not come to Daniel, and could not come to him. What we have from him is now strange. For Nebuchadnezzar he had shown deep concern. He had even expressed the wish that the judgment he was pronouncing from God might fall on his enemies rather than on himself.[1] To Belshazzar he preaches as one standing on the other side of a great chasm. From Nebuchadnezzar he accepts rewards and honours. But before Belshazzar his first reaction is a brusque '*Let your gifts be for yourself, and give your rewards to another*' (verse 17). To Nebuchadnezzar he appeals evangelistically for a change of mind and heart and life. To Belshazzar he preaches a sermon without the trace of any appeal. All he does is to relate the facts that justify the condemnation that has been pronounced in the writing on the wall. Belshazzar knew the truth that might have saved him, and did not obey it.

We can understand what Daniel is doing. He is not there to give expression to his own feelings and thoughts. He is there as he was to Nebuchadnezzar, to bear witness to what he believed was the word and attitude of God. He dared say no more and no less than he did. But can we not believe that he was sick in heart at his own self as he did it, knowing that he too shared the same humanity as was in this wasted condemned life, knowing too that only the incomprehensible grace of God saved him from the doom he was pronouncing on his brother, and praying that God might yet have mercy on this poor man? Belshazzar on his own part was adopting a position and choosing a fate towards which Daniel could not possibly let his heart and mind move with sympathy, and into which he could not enter in the name of God.

The honesty and severity of love

We on our part have to ask ourselves if we can faithfully reflect the truth of God, in whose name alone we can worship and pray and work with people, unless we are willing at times and under certain circumstances, to stand apart as Daniel did, plead from a distance, and offer the same kind of stern warning. There are attitudes, commitments and life-styles which alienate men and women hopelessly from God. We have to remember that even

[1] 4:19.

Jesus was silent when during the time of his trial he faced such a man in Herod.[1] The message of the Gospel to such is not that God reconciles himself to them, or 'identifies' with them where they are, but that he calls them to be reconciled to him and to forsake their ways. Unless they learn to accept God as he is and things as he wills they should be, they cannot hope to come to him and live with him and have fellowship with those who love him.

Therefore we must not judge Daniel too harshly because in his preaching on this occasion he gave no direct evangelistic appeal. We can, rather, admire his daring courage. Just as there appears a 'shadow side' to the Word of God, there must also appear at times a 'shadow side' to pastoral care given in the name of God, and there can occasionally arise the rare case and the rare circumstances in which the pastor, if he is honest, has little else to do but warn.

The church itself has always recognized that along with sympathetic pastoral care and evangelical openness it has also to exercise at times a much sterner discipline. This involves the refusal to condone the flagrant open and persistent defiance of what God loves and has said Yes! to in Christ. It involves stern rebuke against the approval of and persistent indulgence in what God hates and has said No! to in Christ. It involves the command to men and women to desist from such behaviour, and clear and faithful warning about its consequences. The church, in exercising this kind of pastoral care, has sometimes gone to the length not only of rebuking and warning but also of excommunicating people, excluding them from the fellowship of the Lord's table till they express their repentance and willingness to change. The early church put such discipline into practice because Jesus himself taught it, and his words were always quoted:

If your brother sins against you, go and tell him his fault, between you and him alone. If he listens to you, you have gained your brother. But if he does not listen, take one or two others along with you, that every word may be confirmed by the evidence of two or three witnesses. If he refuses to listen to them, tell it to the church; and if he refuses to listen even to the church, let him be to you as a Gentile and a tax collector.[2]

---

[1] Lk. 23:8, 9.   [2] Mt. 18:15-17.

The aim of such discipline was always that the offender would come to a realistic understanding of the truth of God himself, and should ultimately return to him in true repentance, for there can be no fellowship or love that is not also in the truth. At this point that we must look again at Daniel, and at least admit that he is pointing in a healthy and right direction.

The background of the human tragedy

It is deliberately stated that the drinking of wine in front of his thousand guests was a prominent aspect of his feasting, and that it was *when he tasted the wine* that he was emboldened to go farther than, with any sober intention, he might have dared—to call for the vessels from the Jerusalem temple so that he might publicly register his defiance of the God of Israel (verses 1–3).

The Bible does not condemn the drinking of wine as such. It never suggests that alcohol in itself is essentially evil. There is indeed one text which thanks God for 'wine to gladden the heart of man'.[1] There is another which recommends its use to cheer him who is in bitter distress.[2] There is also the fact that Jesus, apparently to save the situation at the wedding party, turned water into wine at Cana.[3]

Yet the Bible much more often warns us that drunkenness is the cause of an immeasurable volume of human tragedy. It makes Noah[4] and Lot[5] shameless and shameful in their family life. It makes Ahasuerus first merry and then cruel and stupid in his treatment of his wife.[6] It brings completely senseless military defeat to Benhadad.[7] It is named by Isaiah as one of the chief causes of social injustice and national doom.[8]

The Belshazzar story underlines all these warnings, and goes even further. At the very moment when everything could have changed, had this man become penitent, his very state of mind and body cannot but have been a contributory factor—perhaps even a major contributory factor—to his inability to respond savingly to the spiritual crisis that was upon him. At the moment when God was giving his final call, he was drunk. Perhaps even his final act of clothing Daniel with honour was a piece of drunken play-acting in which he hardly knew what he was doing. The wine that he has so effectively used to help to cut himself off from life

[1] Ps. 104:15.   [2] Pr. 31:6.   [3] Jn. 2:1–11.   [4] Gn. 9:20 ff.
[5] Gn 19:30 ff.   [6] Es. 1:10 ff.   [7] 1 Ki. 20.   [8] *E.g.* Is. 5:11, 22; 28:1, 7, 8.

and reality, now helps to cut him off from the grace of God.

We will be able more accurately to assess what the Bible says generally about the use of wine if we cease to worry about the question whether it is right or wrong. The Bible does not discuss it under such categories. But in the book of Proverbs many of the big issues of life are discussed in order to show what is wise, what is dangerous, what is foolish and what is fatal. The use of alcohol comes in for a good deal of discussion in this context.[1] It is worth while quoting one of its unforgettable passages:

> Who has woe? Who has sorrow?
>> Who has strife? Who has complaining?
> Who has wounds without cause? Who has redness of
>> eyes?
> Those who tarry long over wine,
>> those who go to try mixed wine.
> Do not look at wine when it is red,
>> when it sparkles in the cup
>> and goes down smoothly.
> At the last it bites like a serpent,
>> and stings like an adder.
> Your eyes will see strange things,
>> and your mind utter perverse things.
> You will be like one who lies down in the midst of the
>> sea,
>> like one who lies on the top of a mast.
> 'They struck me,' you will say, 'but I was not hurt;
>> they beat me, but I did not feel it.
> When shall I awake?
>> I will seek another drink.'[2]

[1] Pr. 20:1; 23:19 ff.; 31:4 ff.   [2] Pr. 23:29-35.

Daniel 6
The den of lions

The mystery of the offence

T^{*his*} *Daniel became distinguished above all the other presidents and satraps, because an excellent spirit was in him* (verse 3). He had something that the others lacked, an extra charismatic 'plus', an endowment from the Spirit of God under whose inspiration he continually did his work. This enabled him often to be 'extraordinary' in the difficulties he could face and overcome. It revealed itself even in tasks that were by themselves quite ordinary. It expressed itself especially in the sheer force of his character, in his attractiveness, the integrity with which he conducted himself in his administrative tasks, and in the uncanny wisdom with which he saw through situations and made practical judgments. This excellent spirit was what Babylon needed. Therefore Daniel drew the attention of most of the kings he worked under and was entrusted by them with top administrative jobs.

They trusted him as if he were a good Babylonian, and in every respect Daniel was completely loyal to his adopted country. He served it with a genuine concern and affection that would have passed the test of any accepted standards. His life-style in many respects was the same as that of those around him. His accent was native and his children could not by any superficial sign have been distinguished from others in the streets. He had done everything possible to qualify himself for citizenship. If Disraeli was an Englishman and Kissinger an American, Daniel was a Babylonian.

But he was hated especially by his peers and fellow statesmen in the administration, and this hatred was cool and determined and bent on his destruction. We can only call it, to use a New

Testament phrase, the 'mystery of lawlessness'.[1] There was no reason whatever why this man should be persecuted and hounded to death, except that he was good, and stood before men as a sign of the existence and grace of a good God. The mystery of iniquity lies in the fact that through the mystery of the freedom given to the creature in its creation to respond in love, liberty and joy to its creator, there has arisen in this universe, created good in all its aspects, a blindly perverse and absurd reaction that can only be called satanic, that has no place in God's original purpose and that can have no place in God's final triumph, though it is allowed to work its strange havoc until the time of its final destruction.

The story of Daniel—hated by his contemporaries, plotted against and condemned to die simply because he stood for the truth, loved what God loved and lived it out—is one of a long series of stories in the Bible of such irrational hatred directed against brother, neighbour or prophet by those who are against God. There is the hatred of Cain against Abel;[2] the hatred of the sons of Jacob for their brother Joseph;[3] the hatred of Saul for David,[4] the hatred of the people of their day against a long series of prophets and messengers of God; and it all culminates in the hatred shown to Jesus in his crucifixion by those who represented mankind.[5]

Anyone who hates his brother ...

The hatred of his fellow courtiers can find its full expression and satisfaction only in the murder of Daniel. This is the case in all the Bible accounts of such hatred; it is always deadly, always seeking to aim the mortal blow. Joseph's brothers meant to kill him. The people stoned their prophets to death.[6] 'Any one who hates his brother is a murderer.'[7] It is the very nature of all true hatred to kill.

It is the crucifixion of Jesus himself that shows us exactly what our hatred is, and what it ultimately issues in as it seeks its fulfilment.

It is essentially directed against God. And deep down in all human hearts all have the same resentment against the truth of God, the same love for what is opposite to God.[8] This opposition finds its culminating expression in the cross itself. We were there

[1] 2 Thes. 2:7.   [2] Gn. 4:1 ff.   [3] Gn. 37:4.   [4] 1 Sa. 18:8, 9, *etc.*
[5] *E.g.* Acts 3:13–15.   [6] 2 Chr. 24:20 ff.; Mt. 23:34–37.   [7] 1 Jn. 3:15.
[8] *Cf.* Rom. 1:25–32; 2 Thes. 2:10–12; *etc.*

when he was crucified, and we were on the wrong side, and when the truth of it all really comes home to us we know ourselves correctly for the first time.

Holy Scripture indicates that hatred itself cannot arise out of the goodness of creation as God made it,[1] but can have its origin only in the intrusion of a satanic mind and spirit and power into the life of this world. It was man's fault and fall and abuse of his freedom that brought him into bondage to this spirit, and it has worked death and havoc everywhere.[2] Its presence is therefore as absurd as its nature is irrational. But its work is real and terrible and gigantic in its scale[3]—so gigantic and devastating, indeed, that God has to put all his strength into a great new reconciling and redeeming act to put things right.

The unswerving witness of Daniel

The story suggests that it was because Daniel was so unashamedly and avowedly godly that he was hated by his opponents. No matter how Babylonian he was in such a large area of his life-style, no matter how loyal in all his main duties to his adopted country, Daniel never failed to let it be known to all around him that what was 'most excellent' about him derived not from Babylon itself, but from Jerusalem, to whose culture and religion he turned constantly for inspiration. Before the eyes of everyone in Babylon he stood boldly and uncompromisingly for this Jerusalem, and for everything it had been built to signify in the service of God. His habit of daily prayer, which he hid from nobody (verse 10), showed to all who knew him where he believed truth was to be found, and where he believed all men everywhere must look for their salvation.

He had windows in his upper chamber that opened *toward Jerusalem*, and there *three times a day* he knelt down and *prayed* to the God who had chosen Abraham and Isaac and Jacob, led Israel out of Egypt and founded the 'eternal city' under David. That city and all it stood for was the lode-stone to which his mind always turned. The orientation of his prayer-closet windows was a symbol of the continual tendency of his mind and thought, when not immersed in Babylon itself, to turn towards everything in his sacred books that spoke about Yahweh and his temple there, the land of which this temple was the centre, the call of the fathers as

[1]Gn. 1:31. [2]*Cf.* Eph. 2:1–3. [3]*Cf.* 2 Cor. 4:3, 4.

they had pilgrimaged towards it, the oracles of the prophets, especially Isaiah, in their visions of its great future. Daniel was certain that one day all people somehow would find their unity by going up to the mountain of the Lord God of Israel.[1] There they would worship God who would speak from his new temple.[2] They would learn to know his law and to walk in his paths, and then they would beat their swords into plough-shares and their spears into pruning hooks, and learn war no more.[3] For Daniel, the future of mankind was bound up not with the great city Nebuchadnezzar had built, but with the one he had destroyed. For him humanity would never rise from the dust till Jerusalem began again to stir. He never ceased to pray that God would restore its ruins, rebuild its walls and take up again the purpose that he believed had been cut off only for a season.

People knew he did it, and they knew why he did it—three times a day! When they asked him what it all meant he was frank in saying what he believed. No true exile was ever allowed by his faith to hide it. Moreover, there were these strange food laws, and these peculiar sabbath-day practices that had become important to the nation now that so much else had been destroyed. Since he had now no temple to go up to in order to witness to the triumph of his God, Daniel opened his windows *three times a day* towards the holy city (verse 10).

But it was precisely this persistent loyalty to the old ways of Judah, this constant refusal to cut himself loose from 'Jerusalem', this repeated claim that the truth and salvation for the world lay there and nowhere else, that made many powerful people in Babylon hate him. They hated him not merely because he was a foreigner and stranger, not merely because they were jealous of his extraordinary ability, but mainly because, in spite of the fact that he was so impeccably loyal and helpful to Babylon, the whole orientation of his outstanding life tended to point not to Babylon but to Zion. Too often he stood simply for what Jerusalem alone stood for. Too clearly his talk and his way of life bore witness to his strange belief that salvation for mankind could come only from the God who had chosen Zion as his dwelling place.

The point of the offence

They could have forgiven Daniel even if he had failed in some of his duties, or even failed to maintain his excellence of spirit—but

[1] *Cf.* Is. 2:2, 3; Zc. 8:20 ff.   [2] Zc. 6:12–15.   [3] Is. 2:3, 4.

107

the idea that the gods of all nations were not really gods at all, that there was no other divine name that ultimately mattered at all, except that of Yahweh of Jerusalem, was something they felt they could not allow to have any further currency in their midst.

It was inevitable that fidelity to the God of Israel in that ancient world should give such offence to those in the surrounding world who believed strongly in the value of their own native religions and systems of thought. Holy Scripture insists that truth is not something generally diffused amongst all nations and races, nor something the natural man by the exercise of his innate abilities or religious faculty can arrive at or think out, but something prepared for, worked and lived out by the living God himself within the context of the life of that one particular nation which he chose by his grace to be a light for all others.[1] The people of Israel, as their history developed and as they became more and more conscious of the power and mightiness of the God into whose hands they had fallen, became also more and more conscious that all other religions were empty and all the gods of the surrounding nations were nothing. In Samuel's time, when the ark of God had been put by the Philistines into the temple of their god Dagon, after the first night the idol was found flat on its face and removed from its pedestal. They set it up again only to find the next day that it was smashed into pieces.[2]

With Daniel, therefore, it was the old story of a man who cannot avoid giving offence because he has come under the constraint of what he believes is the final truth—exclusive and shattering to every other system that wants to exist alongside of it, and utterly intolerant of the possibility that anything else could claim the same finality.

When anyone makes this claim for his religion in the world today he is bound to face the same problems as Daniel faced. Jesus warned his disciples that if they witnessed to him clearly and faithfully and served him loyally they would never be able to avoid presenting the same kind of offence, or having the same shattering impact on a world so rich and varied in its cultural and religious traditions. They would have to preach that he was the Good Shepherd and that all who ever came before him were 'thieves and robbers',[3] that he alone was 'the way, the truth, and the life',[4] that he alone was the Saviour[5] and that all other men

[1]Dt. 4:5-8.   [2]*Cf.* 1 Sa. 5:1-5.   [3]Jn. 10:7-11.   [4]Jn. 14:6.
[5]*E.g.* Acts 4:12.

needed to be saved,[1] that he alone was the good physician, and that all other people were sick and needed him.[2] They would have to insist that truth was that which finally happened once for all time and for all people when he was born in the manger, lived his perfect human life, died to reconcile all men to God on the cross and rose again from the dead.[3]

The injustice of the charge

Of course they could not find ground on which to argue that a man of Daniel's views should be either mistrusted or persecuted or punished. They could not make out a rational or just case against him. No honest frontal attack on this man or on what he stood for was possible. In order to bring him into their mesh they had to resort to a perverted and hidden subterfuge.

The point brought out (in the telling of this incident) in this chapter seems to be that when men bear witness clearly and faithfully to the God of Israel—in their life as well as in their words—the truth of what they are pointing to is unassailable in face of any honest criticism. To all open and rational minds, it bears so clearly the evidence of its own sheer intrinsic worth that men have to turn in perversity against the evidence of their own reason in order to be able to deny that they are being confronted with what is final in the truth about man and God. Only deliberate blind irrationality can refuse to acknowledge the truth.

Daniel, then, could be condemned only by laws that violated basic human rights and that were grossly unreasonable. His accusers had to get the foolish king to make and sign such a law before they could trap their man. After the most searching scrutiny everything about him had remained irreproachable. They had to blind themselves to deny it or to accuse him.

Are we not bound to believe that this remains the glory of what has come to us directly from Jerusalem through Jesus Christ: that no honest man can make an honest case against it, that to hate it and persecute it must always involve to some extent a love of darkness rather than light and an open-eyed rejection of what in itself is always and in every respect 'excellent'? In other words, belief in Jesus Christ involves belief that there is nothing in the Christian faith as it is embodied in the person, actions, or teaching of Jesus that should validly offend the human mind. Only evil and

---

[1]*E.g.* Rom. 3:23.   [2]*Cf.* Mk. 2:17.   [3]*E.g.* Eph. 4:17–21; 1 Jn. 5:20, 21.

perversity can be offended in Jesus. In the true unfolding of this Gospel and its full acceptance by men there is the way and the truth and the life for all men and women for every kind of community, for international affairs, for the future of history, without defect or lack. If true Christianity causes offence it does so only to false human pride and entrenched human evil. To be offended in Christ is to be against truth, humanity and life itself.

A valid analogy therefore can be drawn between the twisted and irrational subterfuges planned by Daniel's enemies to trap him, and what took place at the betrayal and trial of Jesus himself. Every fair legal analysis of the trial shows that everything men had to do to destroy him was in the end palpably unjust. The whole process stank with its fraudulence, illegality, irrationality. His judges had to be cynical, corrupt and weak men. If one important figure in the whole set-up had stood up for what was reasonable and fair, Jesus would have been set free.

Our values and ways are rapidly changing today under the desire to criticize and sift everything unworthy in our heritage from the past. The desire for good change is healthy and often the criticism is just. But sometimes, and especially when the criticism is levelled at the church, the values it has professed and the mission it has often sacrificed itself to achieve, it is sometimes given without valid reasoning, with only a partial look at the facts, and with little attempt to understand the issues in any depth. This takes place because in the upheavals of this age there is not only a spirit that is working good but also a spirit that is out to destroy the good. This is why so often the Christian gospel itself, and the humanity and teaching of the Lord himself, and the best of traditional values that civilization has derived from him and his gospel, are sometimes tragically and perversely distorted in order to be proved despicable, and sometimes openly defied and maligned. We have to be willing to listen to the criticisms of our age, to be open to its often desperate and sincere questioning. But we have also to be aware that human nature has not changed too much since the time of Darius the king!

Murder under the system!

The men who plotted against Daniel did not want to have his blood on their hands. Therefore the question of killing him at a council meeting, each with his own dagger, as the Roman senators did to Caesar, never entered their heads. They did not even try to hire assassins. Their policy was to do the same thing, but in a much more subtle and complex way. Their guileful intention was to wrap themselves in ostensible innocence and to lay the death of Daniel at the door of the innocent king. They adjusted the legal code and its penalties so that Daniel could be condemned to death. They arranged for him to be caught. It was all carefully planned and clearly thought out in every detail. The system would do for them what each would have been too horrified to do by himself—for they were all honourable men!

Then these presidents and satraps came by agreement to the king and said to him, 'Now, O king, establish the interdict and sign the document, so that it cannot be changed, according to the law of the Medes and the Persians, which cannot be revoked.' Therefore King Darius signed the document and interdict (verses 6-9).

It all goes on today—not as the result of such deliberate planning aimed at the destruction of one man, but sometimes as the result of planning and legislation that is careless and forgetful of the rights and welfare of its weakest possible victims, and sometimes because responsible people (like King Darius) remain culpably unaware of the tendencies to harm and corruption that inhere in the new plans and laws they too easily consent to, and thus allow affairs around them to slide into a state that does devastating harm to those who should have been protected and provided for. Thus we have our systems set up by law, and strongly upheld by our establishments as inviolable, which can trap and threaten, as surely as the system in Babylon trapped Daniel, and sentenced him to death. What solves the economic problems of some makes economic slaves of others. What allows some to have their way, pursue their policy, fight their wars and achieve their conquests, brings others into slavery and death. People do not have such a bad conscience about it when the system can be blamed. Therefore we carelessly cast our votes, refuse to call for change or even to criticize, and let the system put people out of work, render them homeless and bereaved, destroy their humanity and decency. If we saw it all happening before our eyes and on our doorsteps we would be appalled and we would refuse to have any personal part in doing such things. It is much easier on our conscience if we can blame the system.

The saving grace of discipline

When Daniel knew that he was being made a victim—that the document had been signed—he went to his house, opened his windows, and gave thanks 'as his custom was'.[1] There is no doubt that what kept Daniel when his trial came was this rigid uninterrupted habit. He had disciplined himself to it day by day for years, and at the hour of crisis the very momentum of the custom itself would have been enough to keep him faithful to it, even if there had been at the moment no living inspirational incentive. Having made the habit such an integral part of himself, he would have betrayed himself as well as his God if he had not opened his windows and got down on his knees.

Often, of course, he found himself immediately refreshed and inspired by what came to him in his time of prayer. The very moment he knelt he found himself spoken to, caught up by the reality of the divine presence and truly and sincerely speaking in living response. His mind became inspired and clarified on the problems for which he sought light. His resolution became confirmed and he went away stronger.[2] But it may very well indeed have been the case that on many occasions the custom brought no immediate satisfaction, and that day after day he did not come away 'blessed'. Was he tempted to feel at times that God must be deaf or sleepy or careless? We know that on one occasion in his old age he became almost desperate to know whether he was being 'heard' and God had to give him a special visit through an 'angel' telling him not to fear because he was really taking note of everything he said.[3] Unless he had deliberately disciplined himself to keep on praying when it became such a matter of routine, he would not have maintained the reality and strength of his communion with God.

Our need of habit

Perhaps this Daniel story gives us a glimpse of the kind of courage, moral stability and spiritual vigour that many of us need, want and lack. We might find ourselves much more free and able to serve God and other people effectively—and we would find our faith becoming a much more real and vital affair—if we were willing to learn something in this respect. At times today we try

---

[1] 6:10, AV.   [2] Cf. 9:3, 4, 20–23; 10:12–18.   [3] Cf. 10:1–3, 12.

desperately to put some pep and reality, spontaneity and creativity into our new forms of worship because everything traditional has become so dull for us. But in the long run we have to learn that the most precious, spontaneous, 'real' and creative things in the Christian life can be given a vital place in our lives only if they are cultivated and protected by discipline, especially in our private devotions. There is no doubt that God sometimes genuinely meets and inspires us and even revives us in the spontaneous experiences that come to us apart from any disciplined routine of private or community religion. But even this new life that comes in spontaneous revival will not last unless it is geared to and preserved within a setting of personal habit, and a faithfully kept church loyalty and attendance can help us to maintain the personal habit. God does not mean us to live on and on trusting in spontaneous revivalism, but rather to cultivate habits of worship and communion with himself. We must quietly, rationally and soberly think out what basic regular and routine habits of discipline, prayer and worship are going to put us always in a reliable way of coming into touch with the reality of God's presence. We must discover what can be relied on to keep us going when things are hard. God himself will revive us again in due time.

But the cultivation of any habit involves taking time from other pursuits, and to cultivate a habit of prayer, worship and devotion such as we see in Daniel could involve us in deliberately taking less time for example in front of the television, less time in bed. It could demand the diversion of our energies from pursuits that come to us and bring their reward much more easily and simply. This is why prayer in the teaching and life of Jesus is often spoken of as demanding persistent and hard effort,[1] and is linked up with 'watching',[2] and why prayer is also frequently associated with 'fasting'.[3]

We have to remember Jesus' own words to those who criticized John the Baptist for imposing a discipline of fasting on his followers. Indeed, when asked about it he said simply: 'Can the wedding guests fast while the bridegroom is with them? ... The days will come, when the bridegroom is taken away from them, and then they will fast in that day.'[4] His word about the bridegroom's being 'taken away' and the forthcoming period of

[1]Lk. 11:1–12. [2]*E.g.* Mt. 26:38ff. [3]Ps. 35:13; Acts 14:23; *cf.* 1 Cor. 7:5.
[4]Mk. 2:18–20.

'fasting' may refer to the whole period between the crucifixion and the second coming. In this case his word would be a call for all Christians to make strict discipline and fasting part of the routine of their normal Christian living. But Jesus may have intended in this word to his disciples also to affirm that the life of those who follow him may be marked by alternating periods of varying mood and experience: sometimes 'rejoicing' because of the nearness of the bridegroom and the felt warmth and strength of his presence, sometimes 'mourning' because all 'feeling' or sense of a 'presence of God' is lacking and the heart is cold and the mind is tempted to be perplexed. In this case Jesus would be emphasizing that at precisely such periods in our lives, our faith can be sustained and kept strong only by the help of discipline and habit. 'If your acts of prayer are the most regular thing in your life,' wrote W. E. Orchard, 'I think you will find that they regulate everything else.'

The law-and-order trap

The final stage in the crime was made possible because Darius, in all innocence, was strong on the issue of inviolable law and order. He believed firmly that this was the secret of all good and healthy government and the only way to prevent crime in a large cosmopolitan society of people of every sort. Such was also the time-honoured tradition of the *Medes and Persians* (*cf.* verses 8, 12, 15).

Rules of conformity were carefully prescribed with much detail, penalties for violation were carefully defined, and when the law was broken the exact penalty was rigorously applied regardless of the variable circumstances of each case. No appeal was allowed, no reprieve could be granted. Not even the king was allowed to grant mercy or make exceptions (*cf.* verse 14).

It was a very simple form of policy. It saved complicated emotional appeals and petitions. It saved rulers from the indignity of having to change their minds, and, of course, it had its virtue especially in a community inclined to lawlessness and permissiveness in the wake of such an administration as that of Belshazzar. It led to respect for government. Darius liked it. Many would have been glad to have this kind of regime when he set it up.

But it led to an absurd situation: Daniel versus law and order!

And tragically too late the king realized that he had made law and order more important than Daniel! '*Know, O King, that it is a law of the Medes and Persians that no interdict or ordinance which the king establishes can be changed*' (verse 15). Daniel, the innocent one, perhaps the best among his trustworthy friends and supporters, was now the victim of his mania for bringing everything under strict and hard regulation.

Darius himself felt as trapped as Daniel was, and he was distressed and *laboured till the sun went down* (verse 14) to prevent what he knew would be a crime. In the end he had to force himself to commit a shameful injustice in the name of his sacred, helpful system of law and order. He had to face the rather paradoxical conclusion that those around him who were zealous advocates and upholders of law and order were also the advocates of the worst injustice he had ever had to push through his courts. He began to see that 'law and order' is a perfect slogan and an inviolable principle only where the system is good and the laws are perfect.

The devil can flourish and work as effectively under the guise of law and order as he does under the guise of permissiveness. When Jesus was crucified his main opponents were the Pharisees and Sadducees, both of them parties strong on the law-and-order issue. The devil can put on a conservative mask as easily as he can put on a revolutionary mask. If he sometimes works successfully in brothels and drinking-dens he can also do some highly successful work in council chambers and police courts. It was perhaps with the realization of this fact in mind that one of the makers of the Gospel tradition remembered the words of an advocate for the crucifixion of Jesus: 'We have a law, and by that law he ought to die.'[1]

The resurrection of Daniel

They made sure that Daniel was put through the same process of execution as every other common criminal, and that *nothing might be changed* (verse 17) because he was of high position and a friend of the king.

But *God sent his angel and shut the lions' mouths* (verse 22), and in the morning when the stone was rolled away from the

[1] Jn. 19:7.

tomb Daniel came out unharmed (verse 23).

For those of us who can and dare believe that this thing happened, the miracle in itself is full of significance. Nothing could save this man except some power that could control the instincts of desperately hungry lions to take their prey when it was thrust before them. And here God gives a sign that even the brute creation is sensitive to his bidding, that he can make the very animals, even if dimly, discern something of his purpose, and more anxious for its fulfilment than the majority of men. The lions acknowledge and obey where humans resist. This is not the first time in Holy Scripture when we are shown or told that when God is at work, animals sometimes act better than humans[1] and we can take what happened as a promise of the coming day when 'the lion shall eat straw like the ox.'[2]

As a picture and type of things to come, the rescue of Daniel from the lion's den was often used in early church frescoes and catacombs to illustrate the resurrection from the dead. Those who regard the book as a tract issued in Maccabean times think that this story was meant especially to comfort those who faced death and the tomb, to remind them of the hope of resurrection even from the underworld and the grave. Expositors in the Christian tradition have felt that the details of *the stone laid upon the mouth of the den*, and *sealed* with the king's *signet* (verse 17), followed by Daniel's deliverance, made this one of the great incidents in the Old Testament's foreshadowing of the resurrection of Jesus himself.

Daniel's experience becomes relevant to us in the quite simple and ordinary situations of a day-to-day life in many and various ways. In the Psalms, deliverance from persecutions and trouble is sometimes described as deliverance from the lions,[3] and we are often encouraged to believe that though our enemies might occasionally set snares for us and trip us up, they will never be finally allowed by God to hold us in their trap.[4] And on an even more mundane level the story at least assures us that if God has such control over the mouths of real lions, he can also control the slanderous tongues of human lions and save their victims.

---

[1]*E.g.* 1 Sa. 6:12; Nu. 22:27; Is. 1:3.　　[2]*Cf.* Is. 11:6 ff.; 65:25.
[3]*E.g.* Pss. 91:13; 57:4–6.　　[4]Ps. 124:6.

Darius

We are not given the same insight into the mind of Darius as we are into that of King Nebuchadnezzar.

The facts are these. He is easily persuaded to issue the first decree which involves Daniel in danger (verse 9). He is deeply distressed when he realizes what danger his decree has involved for Daniel, and he spends a whole day desperately trying to avert the execution (verse 14). He spends the night of the ordeal sleepless and *fasting* (verse 18), and goes to the den as early as possible, inquiring in *anguish* about Daniel's welfare (verse 20). He rejoices in his deliverance, and in one stroke takes revenge on Daniel's enemies and makes a test as to whether the lions were really wild and hungry (verse 24), and issues an impressive *decree* in favour of Daniel's God (verses 25–27).

It is difficult to say what all these facts mean. His signing of the decree in the first place might have been due to pleasure in the flattery that was poured out on him when he was approached with the proposal. His distress and toil in trying to save his victim might have been motivated by pique and anger at having become so easily duped. This would explain, too, the swiftness with which he proved to his deceivers that the lions were indeed dangerous. Yet at least it can be claimed that now at this juncture he is acting in the service of true 'law and order' administered justly for the protection and welfare of the righteous and not merely as an end in itself. And it can be noted that under this kind of 'law and order' Daniel had nothing to fear.

Indeed the all-important fact is that whatever his motives might have been, ultimately Darius protected and upheld Daniel in his high office. The most significant verse in the latter part of this chapter is verse 28: *So this Daniel prospered during the reign of Darius and the reign of Cyrus the Persian.* After Belshazzar Daniel prospered again. The miracle of the lion's den and the openness of the king to judge rightly between him and his jealous enemies brought about a new turn in his fortunes. It indicates how much it now matters, in the divine providential ordering of affairs, and is going in future to matter, that the heathen rulers who have power over the people of God should give them at least justice—even favour—if the promises of God are to be fulfilled. The people of God are going to depend on the favour and protection of others in order to fulfil their destiny, and God is

117

going to demand and see that they get such justice and protection as they are owed. It is the book of Isaiah which almost more than any other Old Testament book brings out this truth. It speaks to Cyrus the Persian in the name of God, calls him God's 'anointed', and appoints him the 'shepherd' and liberator of God's people. He is to help to free them from the Babylonian yoke and send them back to their homeland, and he is to do this even though he himself is a heathen who knows nothing of God.[1] And later it announces to Israel that the kings of the earth will be inspired and led not only to protect and nourish the people of God but to bring glorious tribute (the wealth of the nations) into its life.[2]

What the chapter finally seems to be saying to us at this point is that empires rise and kings come and go, fashions and life-styles change, but the one stable thing in the midst of all this change is Daniel himself—the man of God who does justice, and loves kindness, and walks humbly with his God.[3]

[1]Is. 44:28—45:6.   [2]Is. 60.   [3]*Cf.* Mi. 6:8.

Daniel 7

The beasts and the son of man

A new look at world power

WE now come to the less well-known and decidedly more daunting half of the book of Daniel. It consists of a series of visions very complex in their nature, and often far from clear at first as to their meaning. Scholars debate, more fanciful minds revel in speculation, and the ordinary reader tends to look quickly the other way. Yet all the material is equally part of the Word of God and is able to instruct us for salvation.[1]

In our interpretation of the opening vision of the series we have to keep in mind the date of its occurrence. We noted that the first year of the reign of Belshazzar had deep significance for Daniel.[2] We suggested that this was precisely the time when, after the death of Nebuchadnezzar, he saw the beginning of a deep change in the style, spirit, outlook, and morale of Babylon and its governing classes. He was to find himself forced out of position. He watched as power passed away from those who, when Babylon appeared great and stable, had gathered round Nebuchadnezzar, to those round Belshazzar in the final days of the empire's swift and tragic fall. No doubt those changes could have been a factor in forcing Daniel to think again about the worth-whileness of his life work as a power politician trying to shape the course of affairs in this world. His forced period of reflection on what he had been doing began to reveal to him the dreadful possibilities for development that, for some strange and perverse reason, threatened to possess worldly power and to control the future course of history. It was the same kind of awakening as can occur today when, for example, a nuclear scientist suddenly becomes deeply disturbed by the consequences that could arise and have

[1] 2 Tim. 3:15. [2] See above, pp. 90 ff.

arisen from his research.

Up till this period of his life Daniel would have been justified in imagining that the task of being a politician under any circumstances could be whatever a man wanted to make it. To a good man it could be a noble art. The administration in which he had served had had as its emperor a man of enlightened policies, with a fairly sensitive conscience open to hear protest, and an ability to recognize his own errors[1]—a political boss who had never been able during his later life to forget his famous dream of the fourfold colossus, with its warning about the inevitable triumph of the kingdom of God, and the inevitable destruction of whatever men built to block its progress.[2]

Daniel had ultimately found that co-operation with such a leader brough him into no insoluble conflict with his moral and religious convictions. But the early days of Belshazzar's reign saw a different sort of administration and of court life developing around him. It is not unreasonable to suppose that he took a new look at the business of government, and that he discerned as never before the demonic potential for evil lurking behind all earthly systems of control. He began for the first time to see the underside of world history—the 'Watergate' side—turned up to the surface. He began to become aware that the battle in politics could only too easily be taken over by the principalities and powers of darkness always ready to manifest themselves in history on as huge a scale as possible. He began to see history and politics—and Babylon itself—in a new light.

His interpretation of Nebuchadnezzar's first dream shows that he was already deeply conscious of the sheer vanity that could mark all attempts at empire building.[3] But now in the new and more sombre vision of history that came to him at this stage of his life, instead of seeing, as before, the succession of coming world empires as four deteriorating parts in a magnificent but unstable colossus, he saw them as a series of four filthy and cruel *beasts*, arising out of, and belonging to, the wild slimy *sea* of this world's turbulent life (verse 3)—knowing only such chaos for their origin, and lusting only with an insatiable desire to spread cruelty and further chaos, each preying on its predecessor, and existing mainly to fight and devour. As the whole fearful drama was played out before his eyes his horror mounted, for each succeeding beast

[1]4:34–37.   [2]2:36 ff.   [3]2:36 ff.

became more cruel and more monster-like than its predecessor. The face of humanity was blotted out in the struggle. The first beast alone had some nobility in its bearing and actually stood on its feet, and momentarily took on the appearance of a *man* (verse 4). But the cruelty became more cruel, and the brute force became more uncanny, and the whole culminated in a fourth beast whose savagery so surpassed, and was so different from, that of any wild animal known on earth that no comparison with any is made (verse 7). Whatever escaped its *great iron teeth* was ruthlessly *stamped* to death by its *feet*. Its most grotesque feature was its *ten horns* out of which sprang a *little* horn *with eyes like the eyes of a man, and a mouth speaking great things* (verse 8). Its cruelty was thus shown to be capped by its pride. Had Daniel described it today its eyes would have flashed with devastating radial beams, and its nostrils would have exhaled nuclear poison.

Questions for today

Each age must pose its own serious questions about the worthwhileness of the aims and achievements of its own political life. We noted in chapter 2 that political systems inevitably carry within themselves the seeds of their own decay. Do they also at the same time and in the same way carry within themselves the seeds of such demonic development as Daniel saw taking place in his vision? We cannot forget that even in the New Testament, in the thirteenth chapter of Revelation, we are given a picture of the great beast appearing on the earth, symbolizing the rise of an ultimate anti-Christian government developing to huge proportions within history, urged on by satanic hatred of everything good and Christian and intent on the persecution and extinction of the people of God. Is this what inevitably must rise on the earth as history develops and the natural inner tendencies of those communities and nations that survive in the struggle for existence are allowed to grow for what they are and reveal themselves for what they are? Need our political systems if they survive grow in this way and succumb in this way?

Answers to this question will vary. Some will see more inherent possibilities for good than for evil in the way governments have been constituted by God. Others will tend to feel that the sort of beast shown in the opening vision of Daniel 7 and finally in Revelation 13 is always there, lurking below the surface whenever courts and parliaments meet. For others it will be the vanity and human sinfulness of earthly powers and systems that determines their attitude to civil government.

> Pride of man and earthly glory,
>   Sword and crown betray his trust;
> What with care and toil he buildeth,
>   Tower and temple, fall to dust!

It is, however, clear how Daniel finally answered this question. Even after this dreadful vision he still continued to serve emperors in the most courageous and wholehearted way. This means that he still believed that politics could be neutral, that they need not take on the demonic forms he had seen in his vision. In the New Testament two important pictures of civil government are given. In Revelation 13 it is shown as having degenerated into this greedy devouring beast from the abyss. In Romans 13, however, it is shown as a noble instrument in the hands of God for the development of humanity and goodness and for the restraint of evil. Therefore we need not close the book of Daniel at this point and decide that politics is always devilish, that the United Nations is the Antichrist, that the European Common Market is bound to develop ten horns. 'You are the salt of the earth,' said Jesus to his disciples, 'You are the light of the world.'[1] Salt keeps inherent corruption from taking over. Light tends to keep out the darkness required for evil forces to gather and conspire for mischief. He is telling his disciples that corruption and darkness need not take over (even in politics and administration!) if they are there to give their distinctive witness and leadership. Even Daniel's presence in the system around him, as we have seen clearly in chapter 6, was the guarantee in his day that some element of justice, humanity and truth would not be lacking even among the ruling powers.[2]

The ultimate and tormenting problem

The chapter we are considering, containing the remarkable vision of the four beasts and the ultimately triumphant *son of man*, is in two clearly distinct parts. There is first a description of the vision with no explanation of it (verses 1–14). This is followed by an

[1]Mt. 5:13, 14.   [2]*Cf.* 1 Ki. 18:3, 4; Phil. 4:22.

interpretation by *one of those who stood there*, given in words alone (verses 15–27). This explanation goes into details on certain features which had aroused the curiosity of Daniel. But Daniel got the main message before he turned for this help in further interpretation of the details. Our first concern here will be to show how this vision came to give him the final answer to one of the deep, ultimate questions that never ceases to plague the human mind. It was the question of the origin and destiny of these strange and sinister powers that he now saw to be threatening the good. Where did this evil come from and where was it going?

It is at this point that we find out how deeply even Daniel, though his mind was steeped in Holy Scripture, was also influenced by the strange myths current in Babylon and all round that Middle East area, about what happened before creation. The prevalent belief then was that before this world could be made, the Creator had to exert his control over a wild primeval sea, blown by chaotic winds, and lashed up into continual fury by its dragons and monsters. Some of these are named for us in the Bible, such as Leviathan and Rahab.[1] Since they were supposed by the Babylonians to have power to destroy what was good, the creation of the world could take place only after they were hunted out and destroyed—otherwise chaos and lawlessness would spread as these evil serpents came out and worked their havoc. Therefore the Babylonians had the myth of a continually recurring conflict in which the beasts from this wild abyss were rounded up, conquered and wounded. And they had an annual festival celebrating the recurrence of this fight between their gods and these powers, and the rituals performed at this festival were believed to help the gods in the continuing struggle.

This view of what reality is like is often called a 'dualistic' view of good and evil, whereas the view of the Bible, which is called 'monistic', is that 'in the beginning' there is God himself alone in his goodness and love. The 'dualistic' view is that there is also over against God himself an equal evil force or evil god, so that basic to the constitution of this universe there is an eternal struggle between good and evil.

This is a deeply depressing and pessimistic outlook. To take it seriously would mean that what is pure and good will be for ever under threat, that history has no other course but to go on and on always in the turmoil of a war in which neither side can ever hope

[1]*E.g.* Is. 27:1; 51:9.

for any ultimate victory. Certainly on such presuppositions there could never be an end of evil, since it never had a beginning. Daniel can have been no more immune from the influences and pressures of his environment and the 'spirit of the age' than we are. He can hardly have avoided at least an occasional lapse into Babylonian ways of thought, and this may be part of the background to the severe depression he suffered.[1] Far too many of us today yield our minds too readily to this kind of world outlook, alien entirely to our Christian tradition, and suffer the same bitter consequences. His 'vision', however, brought Daniel back to sanity and truth.

Towards a final answer

Firstly in this vision the universal sovereignty of the God of Israel, before creation, within all history, and to all eternity, is assured. The *four winds* that strive on the *sea* come from *heaven* (verse 2). The sea is stirred and the beasts make their exit under these controlling winds. The scope and period of each beast on earth is limited (*cf.* verses 12, 25). Each is held on a tight leash. The vision brought Daniel in his mind back to the story of creation in the Scriptures: 'In the beginning, God . . .'[2] If he had been living later he would have said, 'In the beginning was the Word, and the Word was with God, and the Word was God.'[3] Here there is no evil, no original sea of chaos—only the Lord!

Daniel's mind is back in Genesis, in a world of thought that points us faithfully to the reality it speaks of. He is back in Exodus, where, at the Red Sea, precisely when earthly circumstances seemed to reflect the old myths, the seas and the evil powers within them present to God not even the breath of a problem.[4] Daniel is back in the world of thought of the great prophets and writers of his own nation, where it is asserted that 'the waters' are always afraid of the God of Israel,[5] that he has dealt decisively and for ever even with Rahab,[6] and can even find amusement in catching Leviathan on a fishook.[7]

Not only is the sovereign control of God over evil asserted in Daniel's vision, but also the wisdom and exact justice of his purpose as leading to ultimate good. The Lord is not only in control, but in wise control. Even within conflict he is taking close

[1]10:2, 3. [2]Gn. 1:1. [3]Jn. 1:1. [4]*Cf.* Ex. 14:13 f., 16, 21–31.
[5]*Cf.* Pss. 77:16; 93:3, 4; 104:6–9. [6]Is. 51:9, 10. [7]Jb. 41:1 ff.

and unerring observation of every agent. He is guiding the steps and ways of those who trust him, and will finally pronounce unerring judgment. As the focus of his vision moved from the chaotic sea to what was above, he saw that *thrones were placed* in the heavenly realm (verse 9). Before any living figure appeared on that scene they stood empty as eloquent signs of hope. When the Lord Judge, with his assessors, comes finally to occupy them, he is one *ancient of days* (verse 9)—a wise figure of a judge, full of understanding and experience. *A thousand thousands served him, and ten thousand times ten thousand stood before him* (verse 10). Each verdict will be heard by all and irresistibly executed. *And the books were opened* (verse 10). The Babylonians believed there were 'tablets of fate' which contained the future all already written up, and, with such an analogy, these books can be thought of as indicating that the future is to be determined not by chance but according to the mind and wisdom of God who has his plans and purposes prepared. These books can, alternatively, be thought of as containing the record of the past deeds of all those who stand around for the verdict—a record written so unanswerably and clearly that no witnesses are required and no pleading can be of any avail.[1]

As the pages of the books were unfolded, the judgment given and the orders issued, the whole scene in the sphere of earthly conflict begins to change. *Fire* issues from the throne to consume the great beast whose very agony and anger stirs him up to further spasms of cruelty and violence; and though there seems to be a prolongation of the havoc caused by the earlier beasts, yet *their dominion* is *taken away* (verses 11, 12).

The kingdom of the son of man

Daniel, because he knew the Scriptures, already knew something of these final answers to the old questions. He is merely being reminded vividly of what he was tending to forget. But in the final phase of the vision there appears as the final answer to his problem something quite new to the whole tradition with which he had been familiar:

> *I saw in the night visions,*
> *and behold, with the clouds of heaven*

[1] *Cf.* Rev. 20:12.

> *there came one like a son of man,*
> *and he came to the Ancient of Days*
> *and was presented before him.*
> *And to him was given dominion*
> *and glory and kingdom,*
> *that all peoples, nations, and languages*
> *should serve him;*
> *his dominion is an everlasting dominion,*
> *which shall not pass away,*
> *and his kingdom one*
> *that shall not be destroyed* (verses 13, 14).

There is a great deal of discussion among scholars about whom this figure of the *son of man* coming in *the clouds of heaven* really symbolizes. Is he simply a divine figure in human form? Or is he a collective personality signifying the people of God, and standing for the fact that ultimately God is going to bestow sovereignty and glory on his oppressed people? (The twenty-seventh verse is used to support this view.) Can this be a vision of the Messiah? Some scholars say no, others, yes. One of the main thrusts of the meaning of the passage is, however, clear. At the end the triumph will not be with the forces represented in the beast-kingdoms with all their inhumanity, but with that which is represented in the 'son of man' figure. The coming kingdom will inevitably belong not to those who believe in oppression and cruelty, whose gospel is blind brute force, whose policy leads to the perversion of what is truly humane and good. The face of man may become obliterated for a season, for one or two generations or perhaps even three, but it will all reassert itself in the end. The son of man will come in the clouds of heaven!

This is surely the final answer. It is the answer of the New Testament. It finds pointed expression in the second chapter of the letter to the Hebrews. That letter was written to people tempted to grow faint-hearted and lose their zeal,[1] having become gloomy and depressed. They had expected to have seen the kingdom of God coming with power in their own day and Christ already reigning over everything! The writer argues that God is one day going to put everything under the 'son of man', and he quotes the eighth Psalm to prove this, insisting that this son of man is Jesus himself.[2] He also admits that in the world of his day,

[1]Heb. 12:3.   [2]Heb. 2:6–9.

'we do not yet see everything in subjection to him'.[1] That was obvious to anyone, for everywhere evil rulers were prospering, good men persecuted; 'the beast' was rampant. 'But', he adds, 'we see Jesus … crowned with glory and honour.'[2] Jesus had risen! Jesus is Lord!—and this, to his mind, was a sufficient sign for anyone in doubt that already he reigns and at the end of all things it is he who will be in full control.

There seems to be little doubt that the reason why Jesus called himself the Son of man so often was that he believed that this son of man figure in the seventh chapter of Daniel referred to what he himself was to do and become. Whatever may have been in the mind of Daniel, it was from this passage that Jesus taught about his second coming and ultimate triumph.[3]

The son of man and the servants of the Most High

At this point our attention is drawn to an important and helpful aspect of the thought of the Bible about the relation of Christ to his people. Each and all of us who live on earth as the people of Christ, belonging to him and united to him, can be thought of as included in him and represented in him. We have first of all to note that in verses 13–14 a single figure comes with the clouds, *one like a son of man*, to whom the kingdom is given. In verses 17 and 27, however, the same kingdom is given not to *one like a son of man*, but to *the saints of the Most High, i.e.* to the people of God. We have the same way of thinking expressed in the book of Isaiah when it uses the term 'servant' of God. Sometimes the word 'servant' is collectively used of Israel as a nation,[4] but the same word is also used of a distinct individual, whom the church recognizes as the Christ.[5]

It has been suggested that these were times when it was natural to speak of a community as a 'collective personality'. But more is involved in this way of speaking than is met by following this suggestion. We find a better clue in the New Testament. Jesus once said, 'I am the vine, you are the branches.'[6] He did not claim to be the trunk merely, but the whole vine. Here is a mystery. The branches are thought of as included in the totality of his person before they are even united to his person.

Paul, speaking of the church and its members, said, 'Just as the

[1]Heb. 2:8.   [2]Heb. 2:9.   [3]*E.g.* Mt. 24:30.   [4]Is. 44:1; 45:4, *etc.*
[5]*E.g.* Is. 52:13—53:12.   [6]Jn. 15:5.

body is one and has many members, and all the members of the body, though many, are one body, so it is with Christ.'[1] Where we would obviously expect him to say 'the church', he says 'Christ', for while to him Christ is always the unique and wonderful individual person who has saved him, he sees that Christ is also a unique man who includes in his own person all those whom he has come to represent and die for on the cross. Paul's way of thinking about this began when he was confronted by Jesus on the Damascus road. He was on his way to persecute Christ's people at Damascus, but he heard Jesus saying to him, not, 'Saul, Saul, why do you persecute my church?', but 'Saul, Saul, why do you persecute *me?*'[2] He expressed the same kind of thought in those passages in Romans and 1 Corinthians, where the first Adam is spoken of as representing and including all mankind in his fall and corruption, and the second Adam, the true man or 'son of man' is also regarded as representing and including in his person all the 'saints of the Most High'.[3]

This line of thinking certainly faces us with concepts difficult to grasp in rational terms (like the Trinity and the incarnation), but it is an aspect of the good news of the gospel in which our faith can rejoice and in which we can find assurance and challenge. For instance, it helps us in living the Christian life if we can grasp the fact that when he died on the cross, we too died in him as he paid the price of our salvation; and that when he rose, we too rose again in him to newness of life and to freedom over all the powers of death and evil.[4] Liberty from evil and sin is therefore ours already because we have already died in him. New life and freedom are therefore ours already because we are thus united to him and included in him. This is the theme of many of these important New Testament passages which we have mentioned. The final words of this vision of Daniel helped to nurture and further the kind of tradition in which Jesus in his own day was able to teach all the more fully and clearly about who he was, what he had come to do, and how he was going to save and help his disciples to become like him.

The haunting details of the last beast

Daniel was told that the four beasts which he saw arising from the

[1]1 Cor. 12:12.　　[2]Acts 9:4.　　[3]Rom. 5:12 ff.; 1 Cor. 15:20 ff.
[4]2 Cor. 5:14 ff.; Col. 2:20 ff.; 3:1-4; Rom. 6:3 ff.

sea were *four kings who shall arise out of the earth* (verse 17). The description of the first beast, humiliated, and then standing upon *two feet like a man*, and being given *the mind of a man*, seems to refer to Nebuchadnezzar (verse 4; *cf.* 4:33, 34), and it is consistent with this interpretation that this first beast is the noblest-looking of all. No attempt is made, however, to say which kingdoms the other beasts signify. Daniel does not seem to have been interested in the second or third kings, but only in the last one. *'Then I desired to know the truth concerning the fourth beast, which was different from all the rest'* (verse 19).

The answer given to Daniel is enigmatic and quite indefinite. It speaks of this beast as *a fourth kingdom* (verse 23), producing a series of kings all ultimately giving way to one different from all the others, gaining his power by treachery, arrogant, blasphemous (verses 24, 25). It is re-emphasized that he so hates God that he cannot resist taking out his spite on those who trust him. It is admitted that he will seem to prevail over them for a season—*for a time, two times and half a time* (verse 25).

Who is the king, and what is the power represented by this beast, and identifiable with such a programme? Everything is simply left vague at this point. A case can be made out that the four beasts must refer to the same succession of kingdoms as are meant in the image of the colossus in the fourth chapter of the book. If this is so, then the succession could be (1) the Babylonian empire, (2) the Medo-Persian empire, (3) the Greek empire, (4) the Roman empire. The little horn would then refer to some great anti-Christian persecutor of the true church arising within the Christian era and within the civilization created by the Roman empire. This would fit in neatly with the interpretation given by the apostle Paul and the book of Revelation.[1] Paul may be understood to expect that the 'man of lawlessness', whom he seemed to identify with the person symbolized by this little horn, was going to develop within the Roman empire of this day, and do his devastating work on earth before being destroyed by Jesus at his second coming.[2] The book of Revelation, too, seems to identify the Roman empire, which was already persecuting the Christian church, with the last beast.[3] Most traditional commentators have followed this scheme of interpretation, and many, of course, since the Reformation, have interpreted the beast as being the Roman hierarchy itself. It is to be noted, however, that in

[1]*Cf.* Rev. 13.   [2]*Cf.* 2 Thes. 2:3–9.   [3]Rev. 17:9 ff.

following up this view we would have to suppose that the little horn of this chapter, since it arises as a development of the Roman empire, is different from the little horn of the next chapter which undoubtedly refers to Antiochus Epiphanes of the Seleucid-Greek empire (175–163 BC).

The ten horns

As for the ten horns, of which three are overthrown to be replaced by the little horn (verse 20), a great deal of imagination has been lavished on deciding which kings or powers these represent. The whole field of the Roman period, which some expositors regard as extending right down to the present day, is so vast and so studded with petty dynasties and rising and falling monarchies that it is not difficult with a little ingenuity to fit these into some historical pattern of events. At the time when Napoleon was thought to be the beast the ten horns and their adventures could be fitted with some careful manoeuvering into the pattern of the kingdoms he himself destroyed and set up again. Equally, when it looked as if the European Common Market was going to include ten members, it excited some expositors of this passage.

But the succession of the four empires could also be: (1) the Babylonian empire, (2) the Median empire, (3) the Persian empire, (4) the Greek empire. This is the view taken by those who look on the book of Daniel as a specially written tract issued at the time of the Maccabean persecution (c. 160 BC). In this case, of course, the little horn refers not to some Antichrist arising out of the Roman Empire, but simply and consistently throughout the book of Daniel to Antiochus Epiphanes.

As for the horns, under this view they seem to refer to kings belonging to the Greek Empire. The field from which to pick and choose nine or ten is here again very wide, for after Alexander's death his Greek empire split into two main divisions,[1] one a line of kings ruling over the region around Egypt (the Ptolemies), the other a line of kings dominating the area of Syria and including Palestine (the Seleucids). No-one can tell from the text whether we are meant to include in the ten a mixture of Ptolemaic and Seleucid kings or whether they are all to be taken from one line of successive kings. When Antiochus Epiphanes came to power (175 BC), he plotted the murder of two of the Seleucid royal house and

[1]See Introduction, pp. 13 f.

one of the Ptolemaics, and these events may be referred to in the description of three horns rooted up and replaced by the little one. The *time, two times, and half a time* (verse 25) could refer to the three and a half years during which the temple lay deserted under Antiochus (169–167 BC).

The need for perspective

We have given a few of the many different views about exactly which succession of empires Daniel was seeing in his vision, and which kings precisely these ten horns are to be held to represent. We do not underestimate the research, thought, observation and imagination of those who spend much time trying to trace these exact historical identities. This kind of study has its own importance. But we must remember that Daniel in this vision saw these beasts and horns not simply as each having its own historical identity, but also as each being a typical example of the kind of empire and the kind of petty satellite power that can and will arise, here and there, now and then, in the field of human history under various different circumstances as time moves on to the fulfilment of God's great purposes with mankind. And he saw, in the strange developments that came about in each beast and that shaped the succession of beasts and horns, typical examples of the kind of development succeeding ages may expect to see occasionally repeated as history moves on to its end. And to him moreover the interaction of beast with beast, and beast with its surroundings, had the same kind of typical significance for history as a whole as well as a more exact correspondence with certain particular historical affairs. Therefore as he reproduces for our eyes and wonderment these strange moving figures to fill the foreground of a vision, he is also telling us to look beyond and to notice that his picture has a rich in-depth perspective. It shows us far into coming ages, so that this little foreground drama of one age can be something of a guide for varied other times—if we will only be willing to see and keep this perspective.

In interpreting the visions, therefore, let us follow in the example of Daniel himself. When he saw four beasts he made a fairly general inquiry about only one of them (verse 19). Let us at first not be too concerned about the exact significance of details, but let us store as many details as possible in our memory. Let us indeed often move as far back from the details as we can, to get as big a picture as possible of the whole canvas. Let us note the lines and movements of the lines in the whole of it, and let us allow the picture to create in our minds also, as it is meant to do, an impression that we have been led to a threshold from which we can look from the age of Daniel himself well into the future and indeed to the end of all ages. In the light of all this we can make judgments about the value and place of things we have read of in our history books, and are reading of in our newspapers. These will be not simply judgments of value, but also judgments about where our own age stands within this great series of movements that are finally to usher in the end of this age.

Reading the signs today

We now have to ask what relevance this detailed description of the last beast has for us, as, from the point where we can catch the deep perspective of Daniel's vision, we look on our world of today. Our task must be to find out where, within the vistas opened up to us, we can trace something that looks very like our present state of affairs. If we can do this it may help us to estimate how near to the end of all ages we really are, or how quickly we are travelling towards it.

There are many today who, after studying Daniel and the book of Revelation, believe that the end of the world is indeed approaching. As initial signs of this approaching end, they look for the appearance of what we might call 'beast elements' in every governmental system on earth which they expect finally to come together and to flower into an anti-God world government. What worries and excites them is not simply the rise of totalitarian governments here and there but also the rise of human associations whose aim is to form central world-wide organisation to give some form of 'world leadership' to each local body. Communistic movements, world-church movements, trades union movements, and common-market movements tend especially to come under suspicion from such serious and sincere Bible students.

We can understand how such fears can arise as we look again at our text. We are certainly warned here of the possible rise now and again of one great beast-government (verse 19), seeking to dominate solely by the possession and use of brute force (verse 20), which is used with manifest self-assurance and bombast (verse 20b) to bring in radical changes in time-honoured laws and traditions and in deeply rooted, humanly cherished customs (verse 25), such changes being forced because the old order stood in the way of self-centred power. And we are warned especially to be on the alert when the venom of this 'beast' is especially directed to crushing the people of God in a long-drawn-out and subtle battle in which their resistance tends to be gradually worn out in weariness and compromise (verse 25).

Of course we all must be on the alert for such signs of the times. But let us be very careful in our comparisons, and let us ask ourselves whether it is indeed a healthy attitude always to be afraid, for example, of great movements, of coming together with others of like mind with aims on a world scale. It is of course a demonic development when people are forced to join in movements and associations, and unions, simply because no free decision or protest against the prevailing trend is allowed, when individual freedom to decide is not respected and the individual is not really heard. Thus people become afraid to resist because resistance is accompanied by persecution and loss. And civil rights are denied. But it is not necessarily a demonic development when a movement becomes great and is able to claim world-wide organization and leadership, when such power has been achieved by free and open discussion and fair methods, and when such power is sustained by the continuing consent of people always ready to re-think their loyalties and give a free response.

We must be careful, therefore, as in the light of this chapter we make our judgments about what exactly is taking place around us today. We are fully justified in reading it as a warning to us to be especially on our guard when the policy of controlling a community involves a deliberate perversion of the truth of the gospel and the control of the church from within so that there will be no resistance to totalitarian plans and programmes. We are justified too, in becoming wary when the powers in control begin to demand for themselves the kind of love and devotion that should be given to God alone. We do not need to look very far for such examples in a world slow to learn the lessons taught to it by the career of Adolf Hitler. Moreover, we need not call it a false interpretation if sincere Christians caught up in the struggles between the great powers, whether in the Far East or Middle East or elsewhere, as they read these chapters of Daniel, name Great Britain, or the USA, or the USSR, or China, as the beast from the abyss engaging in the destruction both of humanity and of the Christian faith. And we need not think it a false interpretation if even within the confines of the continent of Africa we see here and there the signs of the development of a black beast or two, very much after the pattern of the white beasts we have been so familiar with for so many centuries.

Justifiable depression?

It may seem rather strange that this glorious vision of *one like a son of man* coming in *the clouds of heaven* (verse 13)—of the majesty of God, of the knowledge that he was upon the throne unceasingly controlling and judging all things (verses 13, 14)—did not entirely cure Daniel of his depression. His *thoughts greatly alarmed him* and his *colour changed* (verses 15, 28). But Daniel was being realistic. It is a fearful thing to begin to understand the full, present power of the demonic forces that have invaded life, the havoc they can work, and the hell their presence creates for communities and individuals. And is not a like realism needed today? Has the coming of Christ already so completely transformed the situation that we no longer need share such anxiety and mourning over the havoc evil can work?

There are many voices today telling us that since the resurrection of Jesus, the power of evil has been so completely broken that a Christian need never be worried about the extent of its power, and must seek to cultivate a mood of joy and serenity rather than mourning. This sort of reasoning has much that is attractive and persuasive, but it is important that we should consider carefully two aspects of the teaching of the New Testament on this matter. Firstly there is no doubt that evil is a defeated power, and on its way out. Jesus Christ has already defeated the power behind every evil power on this earth.[1] The New Testament puts the matter pictorially for us where it asks us to see that since Christ came, the powers of evil have been cast out of their stronghold in heaven. In the twelfth chapter of Revelation there is a vivid picture of war in heaven and of the devil being cast out on to the earth.[2] This is an echo of Jesus' own claim that because of his work on earth, Satan is falling 'like lightning from heaven'.[3] This means a radical loosening of the hold of the power of evil on this creation, and this is the first effect of the work of

[1]Jn. 12:31; Col. 2:15.   [2]Rev. 12:7-9.   [3]Lk. 10:18.

Christ. And perhaps, if Daniel had known more of the details of how the ultimate triumph of the Son of man over evil was going to be finally worked out, he would not have suffered from such occasional moods of depression, or have allowed his imagination to become so absorbed by the fearful exploits of the last beast and the little horn.

But at the same time as it underlines so clearly the completeness of the victory of the Son of man over the devil, the New Testament stresses the fact that the defeated forces of evil are not yet destroyed and still have power to work havoc and tragedy to an extent that should drive us to prayer, toiling, mourning and watching in 'fear and trembling'.[1] In the twelfth chapter of the book of Revelation the writer affirms that since Satan has been cast out of heaven, he has nevertheless now come down to earth with all the greater viciousness and determination to do his worst before he is finally destroyed. This means that in contrast to 'heaven' now cleared of the enemy, earth will have to undergo a severe time of trial from this wounded enemy in his spite and rage. 'Rejoice then, O heaven and you that dwell therein! But woe to you, O earth and sea, for the devil has come down to you in great wrath, because he knows that his time is short!'[2] Again this is an echo of Jesus' warnings about the increasing severity of the disturbance which will be created by evil powers in every sphere they still occupy as their end begins to approach.[3] Therefore what depressed Daniel is still present in the world today. Evil on this earth can still possess and control individuals, institutions and communities to an extent that never allows us to forget the warning of Jesus himself: 'Watch and pray'[4]—and that gives inevitable point to his beatitude: 'Blessed are those who mourn, for they shall be comforted.'[5]

The need for watchfulness

We can therefore learn something from Daniel—even in his depression. He lived and operated much closer to the realities of earthly government than falls to the lot of most of us, and was therefore fully aware of the dimension of terror inherent in the placing of power in the hands of sinful men. His example can at least warn us to be realistic. We must 'watch' against evil, even as

[1]Eph. 6:12; 1 Pet. 5:8.   [2]Rev. 12:12.   [3]Mt. 24:6 ff., 24 ff.
[4]Mk. 14:38.   [5]Mt. 5:4.

those who are in personal danger. That vision of the beastliness that was involved in his own civil-service administration in Babylon perhaps raised some questions for Daniel about his own part in public affairs. Today we are each of us in danger of becoming far too involved in the struggle for power and wealth and status within present-day society. This struggle itself is often waged with as much beastly ferocity and ruthlessness as took place before Daniel's eyes when he watched the vision of this chapter. If we engage in it, we are apt to become dehumanized in the very process of the struggle, whether we win or lose. Nor do we escape the danger by immersing ourselves in the church. Paul found this same spirit, that creates beastliness and makes beast devour beast, at work in the Galatian church, with its controversies and gossip and judgmental processes, and he warned them that it could lead to their destroying themselves. 'If you bite and devour one another take heed that you are not consumed by one another.'[1] Our Lord warned Peter that the danger he was in because of the temptation of Satan was going to become so severe that his faith would be strained to the uttermost limit, and it would survive only because of Christ's prayers and grace.[2] We must never presume that because Christ has already overcome the devil, the powers we now have to guard against are so weak, and the danger so trivial, that we can act as if life were a picnic rather than still a grim and constant warfare. It is a sphere in which our decisions about which side we are on are still loaded with infinitely serious consequences.

Yet it is significant that the horror of what the beast's development implies was not revealed to Daniel till he had already seen the final triumph of the 'son of man'.

We can thank God that this is the biblical order of things. The real nature of evil powers that ravage this earth, the hell that their existence involves both for humanity and themselves, are never revealed in their full scale of horror and dreadful reality till they are being met by the one who is able to overcome them and save us from them. It is a fact often forgotten that many of the most vivid and fearful features of the traditional Christian picture of Satan, and even of the torments of hell, come from the teaching of Jesus himself. We must not in any way neglect to read that teaching or bypass what it intends to face us with, even though we must never become in any way absorbed in this aspect of the gospel. Towards the end of his life Jesus himself put everything in its true

[1]Gal. 5:15.   [2]Lk. 22:31, 32.

perspective: 'Now is the judgment of this world, now shall the ruler of this world be cast out; and I, when I am lifted up from the earth, will draw all men to myself.'[1]

[1]Jn. 12:31.

Daniel 8
The he-goat and the little horn

The vision—Alexander the Great and Antiochus Epiphanes

TWO particular series of events are focused on in this chapter. Its first striking feature is the sudden whirlwind defeat of the *ram* by the *he-goat* with the sequel in which the he-goat himself collapses (verses 1–8).

The story is told dramatically. As Daniel was considering the ram, noticing its confident display of great strength as it pushed its weight in every direction (verse 4), there took place the most devastating and sudden attack against it from a most unexpected quarter. A he-goat arose *from the west* and simply charged in without any warning (verse 5). Such was the effect of the assault that the great ram was paralysed and fell helpless to the *ground*, to be stamped on and crushed by its conqueror (verses 6, 7).

If the he-goat's conquest was dramatic, his eclipse was equally so. In his triumph he *magnified himself exceedingly* (verse 8). But it was only for a moment. At the height of his confident and exuberant self-affirmation, the noble-looking beast was suddenly brought to an end of his power and into a state of utter humiliation.

Unlike other visions in the book of Daniel, this one allows little controversy over which dramatic feature corresponds to which part of history. Nearly all the commentators admit that the whole vision, so far, refers to the rise and collapse of Alexander the Great. It is clearly interpreted in this way in the text itself (verses 20, 21). The ram who at first dominates the scene and charges triumphantly westward and southwards, scattering everything in its path, stands for the Persian empire. The he-goat with the *conspicuous horn* who made the lightning charge and overcame the ram, only to break its own horn in the effort, stood for

Alexander himself. He won victory after victory over the Persians, attacking at breathtaking speed in a brilliant series of battles from 334 BC on. With ever-increasing momentum he went on as far as India in the conquest of the world of his day: but by 325 BC, at the height of his power, he suddenly collapsed.

As we read on through this chapter our attention is drawn from Alexander to another figure taking his place on the scene before us, coming on after a lapse of some time. First we see the *great horn*, who symbolized Alexander, dissolving into a group of *four conspicuous horns* (verse 8). These are the four generals who took over power from Alexander, and stand ultimately for four Greek kingdoms. Out of one of these shoots forth a *little horn* (verse 9). He is described as *little* because from the beginning of his career there was not a scrap of potential greatness in him. His policies were those inevitably used by nonentities who grasp after power. *Deceit* and *cunning* (verse 25) became his chief weapons. He had to *magnify himself in his own mind* and he resorted to bluster and show. Yet he is spoken of here as a far more dangerous enemy of God's purposes than ever Alexander or the previous Persian emperor could have been, and his rise to power involved the Jewish people in a life-and-death struggle for their survival and success in the service of God.

The little horn was undoubtedly Antiochus IV Epiphanes. It was just before 170 BC, after throwing his little weight about in several directions, that he gained power in Palestine, *the glorious land* (verse 9). Once established there, he devoted himself to the destruction of everything the Jewish religion stood for, his aim being *to cast (truth) down to the ground* (verse 12). When the text tells us that *some of the host of the stars* he *cast down to the ground, and trampled upon them* (verse 10), this is usually interpreted to mean that he deliberately selected the outstanding witnesses of the community for martyrdom, this act being followed by brazen attacks more directly against *the Prince of the host* himself (verse 11). These final attacks against God took the form of edicts forbidding sacrifice and abolishing religious festivals and sabbath observance, and they came to a climax when he placed an armed guard in the temple area, desecrating the sanctuary itself.

He was allowed to work this appalling devastation over a period of some length, *for two thousand and three hundred evenings and mornings* (verse 14), till things could be put right

139

again. Some commentators think this means actually 2,300 days (*i.e.* between six and seven years) and refers approximately to the whole period of the intense persecution of the Jews by Antiochus. Others think that it means, rather, 1,150 days, and refers approximately to the actual time of the cessation of sacrifice in the temple.

A history without a clue—the absurdity of the outcome

If we believe in God, we must also believe that there is some meaning in human history, even though it may be obscure. The things that happen are bound to be so ordered and controlled as to work out ultimately the purposes of God. Goodness is bound in the long run to be vindicated, and wickedness is bound in the long run to be destroyed, and sometimes the reading of history challenges us and even teaches us. When we read over the record of what happened in some place at some distant period, occasionally we can see evidences in the story itself of a divine hand spelling out for us some moral or political or economic lesson for today. When we compare and contrast the fortunes and fates of different societies and different individuals we learn about the way things might go for us in our times, and are led to ask questions about the meaning of life itself.

But if we are left to interpret history with only our own skill, imagination and wisdom, our minds are bound to become deeply disturbed with perplexing questions. Things that have happened have often been so absurd and shocking that we wonder if there really can be any clue at all to any evident purpose in human affairs. We cannot with any certainty think out explanations as to why such a fate happened to one and such a different lot fell to another. The stories of life's rogues are full of unexplainable blessings and the stories of life's heroes are full of unexplainable tragedies. It is obvious that Daniel found it so when he first saw these scenes from history thrown and enacted on the screen of his vision. He was fascinated, for the events before him were fascinating. He was troubled, for the questions they raised were tormenting to his mind. Yet he felt that there must be some deep meaning in the visions, and that they conveyed some divine message to him, for with some fear and astonishment he *sought to understand* (verse 15). And ultimately a clue as to their meaning had to be given to him by an angel. It is worth while, however, before we read on to see what the clue was, asking ourselves what it was about the visions that, in the first impression, must have puzzled and troubled him as he watched the scenes.

The sad and incongruous failure of Alexander at the climax of his career must have given him food for thought. *Then the he-goat magnified himself exceedingly, but when he was strong, the great horn was broken* (verse 8). It was broken by the intensity of the impact that won it astonishing success. Its whole strength had been put into gaining what it became too weak to hold. It put too much of itself into the conflict and its victory was too great. Alexander's fall was due simply to the over-exhausting expenditure of himself and his energy. It was not any fault or imperfection in his effort, but his sheer commitment to his cause and purpose, the sheer brilliance of his success, that brought this end upon him.

A Scottish preacher who served as a chaplain in the First World War put much of his insight and experience into the first sermon of a book he published in 1935. It was called *More than Conquerors* and the author was E. D. Jarvis. He pointed out that though the British seemed to have won their war, nevertheless history showed the usual rule in war was that the conquerors in the end vanquish themselves through this colossal expenditure of effort to win. To be the conqueror is usually so costly that it is hardly worth the effort. This, he believed, was why Paul insisted that in Christ we are 'more than conquerors'.[1] The same Paul in another letter pleaded with his readers to take the whole armour of God for their battle, so that they might not only withstand the evil one in the day of the assault, but also that having done all they might finally 'stand'[2]—so often the victor falls! How often it happens in human history that men and women put everything into some life achievement; the end is good; the effort is full of nobility; the best of their skill and resources are freely given and freely expended; it is magnificent, and they attain exactly the goal they set themselves and even more—but at the moment of attainment everything collapses simply because they have tried too well, given themselves too wholeheartedly. The power to enjoy the achievement when it came has been sacrificed by the colossal expenditure to get there.

Even on quite mundane levels of life we see so much of it. Too often people in academic, business, political and social life put

[1]Rom. 8:37.   [2]Eph. 6:13.

everything into getting there and make an effort that must be called good in itself. And when they have got it—the job, the honour, the degree, the status, the reputation, the fortune—they find so often that in their effort they have done irreparable damage—sometimes to home and family relationships, sometimes to health, sometimes to their own personal ability of heart and spirit to settle down to enjoy anything in a simple and wholehearted way, sometimes to their power to appreciate quickly the new opportunities that now offer themselves in abundance. They find something has snapped—like that great horn in the vision—and they have finished themselves.

Possibly, for Daniel, the ironic contrasts drawn in the visions between Alexander and Antiochus Epiphanes were as saddening and perplexing as the personal tragedy of Alexander. The latter may have had many defects of character, but even in the briefest account of the great achievements and changes that have taken place in human affairs, involving military campaigns, Alexander's would have to be singled out for special mention. And in comparison to Antiochus, here, he is shown as having not only some greatness but also some honour. Whereas the previous chapter of Daniel described the conflicts of history as usually taking the form of a struggle between slimy beasts rising out of the abyss, the conflict in which Alexander took part is here described as a trial of strength between two much more noble-looking animals. Honour is given where honour is due.[1] With all his brilliance as a general and leader, Alexander must also have had some other admirable qualities of character, for he displayed extraordinary power in the face of impossible difficulties and won through to final triumph. In this he is made to stand in contrast to the *little horn* who followed him and who gained his power and success solely by virtue of trickery and guile.

We are surely meant to see, as Daniel must have done, the bitter irony of the thing—the contrast between the way each came to power, and the fact that at the point where the great and noble man failed, the mean and cunning man prospered! Antiochus shows us an easier way than Alexander to achieve our end in this life and to survive to enjoy what we achieve. That is to practise sordid policy and cunning rather than to spend our strength in open honest conflict. Antiochus succeeds and enjoys his success for so much longer than Alexander. He really gets what he wants,

[1]Rom. 13:7.

and that with nerve and energy intact. When he achieves his goal on earth he is able to sit back and plan how far he can start attacking heaven itself—and he is allowed to do a great deal of damage, even in that direction! All this is to be done by a very little man, with not much ability in straightforward encounter with his peers, but he is an expert in what is below the surface, in what is underhand and twisted. And though he has not much prowess, he has plenty of boastfulness and brass neck. He deceives and then surprises his victims—especially those who rely on things being open and above board.

As he thought about all this, Daniel may have reflected, too, on the irony of the fact that Antiochus' success was made possible only because Alexander pioneered his way for him. The irony about the career of this little man of cunning and subterfuge is that he is able continually to capitalize on the achievement and work of his great predecessor. It is sometimes in the wake of the brave and the good that an entrance is made for the rogues and the robbers. The pioneer work of a Livingstone opened up some of the continent of Africa to slave traders and drink-pushing profiteers. A country can be led for a time by wise generals and heroic patriots who achieve new liberty for the people and new opportunity for building the great new society, but ultimately they let the government fall into the hands of little men, without ideals or courage or true vision, who are only out for their own aggrandisement and profit.

In the character of Antiochus Epiphanes, there were no noble qualities to explain how he became so great. He achieved his power by giving favour to any who would betray their friends and allies, and to those who had no scruples. Even when he got to the top, he behaved as though he were still in the underworld. Of course he is broken in the end, for there is an end to everything on earth as it is. But he had a long and 'successful' career. And it is of him and those like him that an acute observer of history, long before Daniel, wrote in his meditations:

I saw that under the sun the race is not to the swift, nor the battle to the strong, nor bread to the wise, nor riches to the intelligent, nor favour to men of skill; but time and chance happen to them all ... There is an evil which I have seen under the sun, as it were an error proceeding from the ruler: folly is set in many high places, and the rich sit in a low place. I have seen slaves on horses, and princes walking on foot like slaves.[1]

A foretaste and foreshadowing of the final Antichrist

It must have brought some relief to Daniel in his perplexity to hear the angel-interpreter telling him that the vision was *for the time of the end* (verse 17). Only when he understood the kind of end, or climax, that history was moving towards, would he be able to understand the vision.

It is helpful to recall at this point the thrust of the prophetic vision already recorded by Daniel in chapter 7. It is there suggested that towards the end period of human history, just before the kingdom of God finally comes, there is to arise out of the maelstrom of the conflict among the nations a figure of infinitely sinister importance. In a last, desperate attempt to spoil all that God has done, he is to instigate and lead people to an ultimate rebellion against God's will. He will attempt to dethrone God himself and scatter the hosts of heaven. This one is to be the final Antichrist, and the time of the end is therefore to be a time of great conflict. The demonic forces that have arisen out of the abyss, and have embodied themselves in a world power, and allied themselves to this Antichrist, will engage in a titanic struggle against the truth and power of God and those allied to him.

Now, in this present chapter, at this point in his apocalyptic education, Daniel is asked to see this final Antichrist embodying himself in this obscure but pretentious Greek monarch. The same demonic powers that in the latter vision are seen to rise out of primeval chaos, and in the end will vaunt themselves so boldly against God on high, are here seen to ally themselves, during the course of history, with any petty little earthly ruler or administrator or ecclesiastic who is dirty enough to sell himself in their service. They will stoop to use even little Antiochus Epiphanes IV as one of their chosen instruments and means of expression! And it is because of his allegiance to such powers that this little man, so insignificant in himself, so mean and cunning, can do a work that seems to have such greatness. Moreover, if the commitment is close enough, these powers can reproduce even within such a small compass all the signs and symptoms and disturbances that will manifest themselves at the final end.

The spirit that possessed Antiochus, therefore, and allowed

[1]Ec. 9:11; 10:5.

him to achieve his earthly success, is the same spirit that will inspire the final Antichrist in the last days. When the people of God in the second century before Christ were made the target of this earthly ruler's spite and cunning, they were suffering under a hatred far more intense, deceitful and determined than is the normal fate of a historically enslaved people. They were indeed suffering as the immediate and ready target of the powers of evil that hate God's work and are out to destroy for ever whatever confesses his name. They were being attacked by a typical Antichrist even before Christ came in the flesh! Daniel was thus able to attach a unique importance to this little figure, Antiochus Epiphanes, arising so dramatically out of the Greek dynasty, whose career had such a baneful effect on the life of the people of God that he could dominate their official rulers, desecrate their sanctuary and cause even sacrifice to cease—he was a sign and symbol of what is to come at the end.

They were fearful days for those who fell into the clutches of this persecutor, and those who remained faithful and yet survived found it hard to hold on to their faith. *His power shall be great, and he shall cause fearful destruction, and shall succeed in what he does, and destroy mighty men and the people of the saints. By his cunning he shall make deceit prosper under his hand, and in his own mind he shall magnify himself. Without warning he shall destroy many; and he shall even rise up against the Prince of princes, but by no human hand, he shall be broken* (verses 24, 25). There he stands, there he expands to dreadful greatness, and apparently no human force can bring him to an end. We cannot blame the people who lived through these days for believing that history could not last much longer and that the end of all things must be imminent.

We are being warned that the same kind of thing can happen in our own day, the same kind of spirit can embody itself now and then, here and there, in this and that, all with such success that Christian people can imagine the end of the world to be already at hand with all the features that are to mark the last days of the planet earth. We must be on our guard, ready to judge with discernment every new movement around us, especially those which make pious claims. We must be sober, and not imagine too soon that this really means the end of the world. We must be confident, knowing that there is a non-human hand that has already broken the power of such an Antichrist. We must at the same time be deeply troubled, as Daniel was, and yet even in our trouble get on with the work in hand (verse 27).

Back to the king's business!

The experience of this particular *vision* made Daniel physically *sick for some days* (verse 27). Even after he managed to stagger on to his feet and back to work it remained with him and for some time *appalled* him. Psychologically for a period he was deeply depressed and unhappy. He could no longer remain content with the superficial sense of well-being and happiness that up till now he had tended to cultivate. He felt that now he had to find a new way of living victoriously with deeper unanswered questions than he had hitherto faced, with a conscience more sensitive to the rights and wrongs of history, and with a greater burden of sympathy for the victims of its ways and tragedies. His reaction to its sordid side was simply one of sheer horror, devoid of all morbid interest. We will find in the next chapter that all this pressure drove him to seek God by prayer and supplications with fasting and sackcloth and ashes.[1]

Daniel was burdened because he was near the truth. At this point, as at many others, the book of Daniel helps us to understand the teaching of the book of Ecclesiastes:

> And I applied my mind to know wisdom and to know madness and folly. I perceived that this also is but a striving after wind.
> For in much wisdom is much vexation,
> and he who increases knowledge increases sorrow.[2]

It is noted, however, that Daniel, even at this testing period, allowed no permanent place in his make-up for any kind of cynicism; it was only *for some days* that he let the burden of his thoughts sicken him. Then, he says, *'I rose and went about the king's business.'* He is always ready for action and always with strong hope. At this very time the king was Belshazzar and the *king's business* was the kind of minor government post to which rulers relegated people they wanted to forget. Daniel put himself into the work for the sake of God and the future he believed was there—even for Babylon.

[1] 9:3.   [2] Ec. 1:17, 18.

Daniel 9

A prayer and a prophecy

Daniel, the community and the books

HERE we are given our first glimpse of Daniel poring over what he calls *the books* (verses 1, 2). We have seen that three times a day he opened his window towards Jerusalem, but there is not the slightest doubt that as frequently he opened these books—the scrolls that the exiles had been careful to bring with them from their homeland, and to copy out for each other's use. It is obvious as we read carefully through the account of his life that his religion was much more radically book religion than it was vision religion. The dominant laws of his life are basically those of the books. When we listen to his praying, the spontaneous utterance of his heart is expressed simply in a series of subtly woven quotations from those books which have become such an intimate part of himself.

For the whole community in Babylon it was the books that kept their tradition, theology and worship whole, alive and faithful. They had no temple. They certainly had some living prophetic voices who could bring them a direct and fresh word from the Lord. But their main inspiration came from reading, studying, and interpreting their Holy Scriptures. A recent Old Testament scholar, describing life in the villages in which most of them had to settle, suggests that they carried on their own internal government through their own system of elders:

> In these villages of colonists, exiled priests would naturally assist such religious activities as might still go on (*cf.* Ezk. 8: 1; 14: 1), at places of prayer by the waterside, or at meetings conducted by men learned in the scriptures, or in their own

houses (*cf.* Ps. 137 and Acts 16:13).[1]

After some years in exile they could still be challenged to faith and action in the name of a God of whom they were expected to be sure because they had been 'told' about him, no doubt in such meetings together.[2] This kind of gathering may later have developed into the synagogue worship and instruction with which Jesus himself was so familiar.

The books and the presence of God

Daniel tells us first of all that he sought in the books some light on the problem of Jeremiah's prophecy that the exile was to last for seventy years.[3] As the date for return seemed to be getting nearer, he was concerned to know more. From when did Jeremiah mean the seventy years to be calculated? What other words of Scripture could help in interpreting his prophecies?

But the books meant much more to him than a means of answering his problems about dates or theology. He believed that as he sought in them the Word of God, he could be brought through them to experience God himself. *'Then I turned my face to the Lord God, seeking him by prayer'* (verse 3). With the books open before him, his life is oriented towards the living God, and he is given the same confidence in prayer as he used to experience in the temple of Jerusalem.

We may well believe that this could have been the experience of all the exiles, and it may have been one of the greatest fruits of the exilic experience that as they turned to the books they found God himself drawing near. They had missed the temple especially because they had found that its ritual and teaching and sacrifice had brought them communion with God. Their prayers and psalms spoke of their seeing the face of God in that temple, of 'coming into his presence' there. Then in exile they had at first felt cruelly cut off from such access to the presence of the living God himself, and deprived of so much they had held so dear. But as time went on they discovered that the 'books', by the grace of God, were bringing to them what the temple could no longer bring. They seemed now to have, through the books, an intimate way of turning to God himself, of seeing his very face and presence

[1] W. Eichrodt, *Ezekiel* (SCM Press, 1970), p. 53.   [2] *Cf.* Is. 40:21, 28.
[3] Je. 25:11; 29:10.

without being disappointed. The 'books' became for them the place of encounter with the living God himself. And as they listened and read, either in community or even alone, they found themselves listening to the same living voice as their prophets and priests had so often claimed to hear and bring them, and it comforted and challenged them with no less power and relevance than it had had in the lives of their forefathers and mothers in the faith. In this way they were allowed as a nation to discover what today is always a new and wonderful mystery—that God has tied up real and living religion so closely with the Bible.

Of course, Jesus himself insisted that our religious devotion must centre always in himself as the way to the Father and as the one who reveals the Father, and that our Christian service must always find its inspiration in his personal leadership and command. This is what he meant when he said such things as, 'Follow me,'[1] 'I am the way, and the truth, and the life,'[2] 'Unless you eat the flesh of the Son of man and drink his blood, you have no life in you.'[3] For us this means that today there can be no finding of God that in any way bypasses his humanity, or substitutes something else for himself. There can be no following of duty, or acceptable service, other than in the basic pattern and attitude marked out for us in the way of life he took when he was on earth; and there can be no experience of life in the Spirit, be it ecstatic or mundane, enthusiastic or pedestrian, which does not reduplicate within us the life that was in him. He stressed all this especially in a word he once spoke to Philip at a critical time in the latter's life. Philip had obviously been to some extent unsatisfied with what his experience of three years with Jesus had so far brought him. It had not led him into the same kind of vision of God that Isaiah had had in the temple,[4] or Moses in the cleft of the rock,[5] or Ezekiel in his exile.[6] He was restless with the thought that Jesus might now be going away to leave him before he had attained to such visionary certainty. 'Lord,' he said to Jesus, 'show us the Father, and we will be satisfied.'[7] It was a sincere cry for reality in his life with God. Jesus' reply to Philip half-concealed his deep disappointment, and must have been to some extent shattering: 'Have I been with you so long, and yet do you not know me, Philip? He who has seen me has seen the Father.'[8] Philip

---

[1]Jn. 21:19. [2]Jn. 14:6. [3]Jn. 6:53. [4]Is. 6:1, 2.
[5]Ex. 33:21-23; 34:5-8. [6]*E.g.* Ezk. 1. [7]Jn. 14:8. [8]Jn. 14:9.

must now take more seriously than ever he had done the man before him, into whose friendship and service he had been called and from whom he had not yet taken the best that he had come to give. He must watch him so that he could begin to see and receive what was really there to be seen in this humanity and received in this presence. He must keep in close touch with him now, especially as he went out to lay down his life finally on the cross. With Jesus on the scene, all other ways to attain heavenly vision or fuller religious experience have been cancelled. 'Blessed are your eyes,' he once said to the same disciples around him, 'for they see, and your ears, for they hear. Truly I say to you, many prophets and righteous men longed to see what you see, and did not see it, and to hear what you hear, and did not hear it.'[1]

The search today

But how are we today to find in Jesus what he was challenging Philip to seek so intently in himself? How can we today possibly interpret for ourselves his invitation to 'eat the flesh of the Son of man and drink his blood' so that we may have life through him? Such a quest is bound to involve us in nothing short of what Daniel did when he pored over the 'books'. It no doubt also involves us in partaking of the Lord's Supper, for Jesus may also have been referring to the sacrament when he spoke of eating his flesh and drinking his blood. But in their most challenging and direct meaning, his words refer us to seeking the 'flesh and blood' of his humanity in the place where it is most clearly and simply presented to us, and that is in Holy Scripture. For us, to 'eat his flesh' and 'drink his blood' must mean the study of the Gospels in their setting at the heart of the Bible, and we can thank God that our 'books' are much more complete and clear in their witness to him than were those that Daniel had before him in Babylon.

We are passing through a time in our church life today when somehow quite a number of people are expressing disappointment with what they have found so far in their religious pilgrimage, and are being tempted to bypass the 'books' and thus the humanity of him to whom they give their witness. Some are being too easily led on by the belief that the secret of ultimate assurance in the Christian life can be found in some spiritual experience of ecstasy or inspiration not necessarily directly

[1]Mt. 13:16, 17.

connected with the Word of God. Others feel that vision religion does seem to offer much more excitement and reality than what they imagine is more book religion. Daniel in this chapter shows us a more excellent and certain way.

Let me tell one story of my life [said Dr Martin Niemoller once at a meeting of the National Bible Society], of how I came to know what this book is worth. It was on the 2nd of March, in 1938. I had been in prison in Berlin for eight months and had been tried. After the trial I had been taken by the Secret State Police and they had put me in a van, and had brought me to a concentration camp north of Berlin. They took my wallet, they took my wrist watch, they took my wedding ring, and they took my pocket Bible, which I had been allowed to have with me during the days and weeks and months in Berlin prison. This first night I shall never forget, because I didn't sleep for one minute. I didn't find any peace. I was quarrelling with God and blaming Him. I had lost my memory during the very strenuous weeks of the trial. I couldn't remember a single verse from the Book by myself. I was dependent on what was printed. I assure you I should gladly have given not only eight oxen but years of my life if only I could have had that Book. Next morning, when the commandant entered, I asked him, 'Let me have my Bible back.' The man wavered. I was the personal prisoner of the Fuehrer. If he treated me too harshly it might be bad; and if he treated me too well that might be bad also. In the end he turned to the orderly and said, 'Go over to my office and bring the book which is on my desk. It is the Bible; you bring it here.' I had not yet been for twelve hours in the concentration camp and the Book had entered—the Holy Bible—the Book that bears witness and testifies to the One to Whom all power belongs in heaven and earth, even in concentration camp. There the Book was, and there He was with all His strength, with all His comfort, with all I needed.[1]

The presence, the books and the prayer

And now with the books—and the presence of the living gracious God—what can Daniel do but break out into more prayer—into a flood of prayer that was simply part of the happening? '*Then I*

[1]*Report of the National Bible Society*, October 1959, p. 9.

turned my face to the Lord God, seeking him by prayer and supplications with fasting and sackcloth and ashes. I prayed to the Lord my God and made confession' (verses 3, 4). The prayer follows, tumbling out into verse after verse, till it almost seems as if Daniel had forgotten about the date of the end of the exile.

We can note the predominance of *confession* in this particular prayer (verses 5, 6, 11, 14, 15). When men and women come into the presence of God, this is nearly always the first thing that pours out of them. The presence of God means the presence of holiness, in face of which people always feel sinful. Isaiah felt just like Daniel when, in the temple, he too met God. The only words he could utter were a cry of pure confession, from an experience of deeply felt abasement and *confusion of face*. 'Woe is me!' Isaiah cried, 'For I am lost; for I am a man of unclean lips, and I dwell in the midst of a people of unclean lips; for mine eyes have seen the King, the Lord of hosts!'[1]

Daniel's prayer contains a lot of what he calls his *supplications* (verses 3, 17, 18, 20, 23). This simply means that he asked God for what he felt he needed most. He asked for himself and others the forgiveness and deliverance that was the cry of his heart. *'I prayed'* means 'I asked'. How could he fail to ask—when the face of the Lord God which he saw at this moment was the face of the gracious fatherly saviour of Israel? We may be sure that we are genuinely in communion with God only if this 'presence' inspires us to ask in the way Daniel did—to ask about the fulfilment of his promises in our need, and to ask passionately. For God is a God who wills that his people should live before him and serve him in the strength that always comes by asking and receiving.[2] This is what we mean when we say he is a gracious God and claim to live 'by his grace'. God seeks fellowship with us as the Father who wants his children to be always asking for what he promises to give. It is sometimes said that we should think of prayer not as a means of 'asking' for things but rather as a means of communion with God. It is true that fellowship with God is an important aspect of prayer. But in genuine Christian prayer we have both the fellowship and also the asking.

---

[1] Is. 6:5; *cf.* Jb. 42:5, 6; Gn. 18:2; Dn. 9:8.
[2] *Cf. e.g.* Is. 30:19; Ezk. 36:37; 1 Ki. 3:6; Lk. 11:9.

An individual in community

Like the Lord's prayer itself, Daniel's prayer is a 'we' prayer even more than it is an 'I' prayer. He is presenting not only his own personal confession and supplications but also those of *our kings, our princes, and our fathers, and ... all the people of the land* (verses 6, 8, 16) as if they were his own. His burning concern is not mainly for himself but for the religious community, the nation he so deeply belonged to in heart. The reading of the books made him feel acutely the burden and shame of all the people of God—the shame that they should have treated God with such wilfulness and disobedience, the shame that instead of prospering and following God's purposes and witnessing to his glory, they should be in such a state of humiliation and impotence. As he read all this in the books before God, and let it sink in, his prayers simply re-breathe the heart-passion and longings of those who followed Abraham and Moses in the way of intercession,[1] and take up again and re-echo the lamentations and prayers and confessions that had been prayed by other men before him— prophets and psalmists, kings and commoners who down the centuries were moved by the same concern, the same perplexity, the same shame about Israel and about all God's world.[2] Living in depth with the Bible, we too can find ourselves caught up in its passion and concern for men and women who are living without God and who are sometimes forced to live without love and justice, for humanity, and for the world, and indeed for the whole of the natural creation. Thus we become delivered from our self-centred individualism. Living with the Bible makes us community conscious, church conscious, conscious of our brother and his need, and we spontaneously and genuinely begin to pray for others as we pray for ourselves.

Yet Daniel's prayer is uttered also with intensely felt and real individual concern before God. Of all the great figures in the Bible he is probably the one most often solitary, and in praying this prayer he is alone before God. It is as much the genuine and passionate utterance of an individual soul as any other prayer in the whole book. His own personal need is involved. His own heart is being genuinely poured out to God in an intense I-thou

---

[1]Gn. 18:22 ff.; Ex. 32:31, 32.   [2]*Cf.* verse 4 with 1 Ki. 8:23; Dt. 7:9, 12. *Cf.* verse 5 with 1 Ki. 8:47. *Cf.* verse 6 with Je. 6:4, 5; 44:4, 5; and *cf.* verse 7 with Ps. 44:15; Je. 7:19.

relationship. He is seeking *his* forgiveness, *his* deliverance, *his* God. Such genuine individual religion always goes along with genuine community religion in the Bible.

Reality and liturgy in the Bible

Daniel found in his experience that the very language of the prayer itself rose from the books. His prayer is what we could call 'liturgical.' It is made up of a mosaic of phrases taken from all over the books he had been studying, and inevitably memorizing. There is no attempt on his part to address God in the language of a Babylonian exile of the sixth century BC. He used what had become the common language of the people of God from centuries of use. One or two scholars actually reject the long prayer section in this chapter as not being genuine. Their reason for doing so is that it is written in much better Hebrew than the rest of the book. But perhaps the reason for the difference is simply that Daniel's prayer language was dominated by what he found in the books.

This glimpse of Daniel's prayer can help us in some ways. We have already pointed out[1] that we must try to pray, often when we do not feel like doing so. But if we first turn to the books, as Daniel did, and find that they are presenting us not with the dead letters of an ancient text but with a living voice—with words taking life—then it will not be so difficult for us to begin to speak in response to the promises and challenges we are hearing already. This will be especially true, for example, if we read passages from the Gospel story itself before we try to pray, or passages from the New Testament letters, and realize that the kind of thing Jesus did for others in his day on earth, he wants to do for us in our situation. We must try to hear his living voice giving us the same promises and invitations as he gave to the desperate and sick around him in those days, and which the apostles re-echoed in their writings about him.

It is true that even when we use biblical language to give shape to our prayers we can be in danger of slipping into a too-easy formalism, and of uttering prayers that have become a heaping up of 'empty phrases'.[2] Such a fall into insincerity can take place even in our use of hymns in the church, and no-one expressed more cogent warnings against such a practice than John Calvin:

[1]See above, pp. 114 ff.   [2]Mt. 6:7.

Unless voice and song, if interposed in prayer, spring from deep feeling of the heart, neither has any value or profit, in the least with God. But they arouse his wrath against us, if they come only from the tip of the lips and from the throat, seeing that this is to abuse his most holy name, and to hold his majesty in derision.[1]

Our prayers must, then, either themselves arise from the heart or be such that they can carry the heart along with them as they are uttered. There is no doubt that as they arise from the heart we will often find ourselves praying simply in our own words as we pour out our desires and devotion to God. Genuine prayer will therefore always tend to break through liturgy and formality. But a long-drawn-out experience of participation in up-to-date 'experimental' worship has taught me that when the need arises to select or prepare and use the prayers in personal devotion or common worship, then the prayers which use the language of the Bible are more likely to carry the heart with them than many of the studied attempts to coin fresh and non-biblical devotional phrases in what often seems to become a rather pathetic attempt to speak sincerely to God. We must never forget that Christ's own prayers were shaped and cast in the same devotional language and Old Testament phraseology as that of Daniel himself. His own prayer life was nourished through the repetition of the traditional confessions and petitions, supplications and thanksgivings of the life of the people of Israel—and the Spirit who must inspire all our prayers comes from him. A pioneer missionary to Mongolia wrote this, a short time before he died:

> When I feel I cannot make headway in devotion, I open the Psalms and push out my canoe and let myself be carried along on the stream of devotion that flows through the whole book. The current always sets toward God and in most places is strong and deep.[2]

Dates—or assurance?

When Daniel started praying that day his mind had been set on knowing one thing, asking one question: What date had God

[1]*Institutes*, 3.20.31.
[2]James Gilmour in a letter to Mr Owen, 29 December 1890, quoted in R. Lovett, *James Gilmour of Mongolia* (RTS, 1895).

really fixed for the return from exile? But reading the books and the realization that he was in the presence of God forced him to get his priorities right. Therefore he soon began to forget about the dates in the diary of God and found himself troubled in mind about a much more important and basic issue: could there be any hope of return at all for a people with a history and attitude like theirs? We have seen that his prayer about this matter is very long—one of the longest recorded in any narrative section of the Bible. It is a cry from the heart simply for the assurance that God will not allow his people's sins to separate them from himself. The question that burdens his mind is raised again and again in all the varied forms taught by Old Testament practice in worship. Can God possibly forgive such a crowd with such a history? Can God really take seriously the prayer of a member of such a community? How could he presume to go to God with any other problem if this basic question of life or death still remained unsettled?

But the question of the arithmetic of Jeremiah's prophecy still remained there in his mind, and God answered him in a remarkable way. An angel appears with a fully prepared lesson on the secret of the dates, periods and movements of future history. But this lesson comes last in order, and is given only after a very remarkable and beautiful word assuring the forgiveness he was so desperately seeking. The answer to the question about numbers is called the 'prophecy of the seventy weeks'. We shall deal with it in a separate section. It raises so many new difficulties and is itself so full of ambiguities that we have the impression that God wishes to assure his people about the future without allowing them to become preoccupied with calendar matters. But—as if to encourage us all to get our priorities right and always to centre our prayers on the important issue, the cry for assurance is answered freely, with glorious certainty and fresh insight.

'While I was speaking and praying, confessing my sin and the sin of my people Israel, and presenting my supplication before the Lord my God for the holy hill of my God; while I was speaking in prayer, the man Gabriel, whom I had seen in the vision at the first, came to me in swift flight at the time of the evening sacrifice. He came and he said to me, "O Daniel, I have now come out to give you wisdom and understanding. At the beginning of your supplications a word went forth, and I have come to tell it to you, for you are greatly beloved"' (verses 20–23).

'Fear not . . . I have called you by name, you are mine.'[1] Daniel heard himself addressed, as Moses and Abram, Isaiah and Jeremiah before him, by his personal name. Nothing could have been more deeply assuring. But whereas Moses and Abram were called 'my friend', Daniel is 'greatly beloved'. He is assured that from the moment he began his prayer (*At the beginning of your supplications*, verse 23) he was heard. Obviously he had had questions, as many of us do, about how far his prayers were really being listened to. He is thus given assurance about the worthwhileness of his praying even before he is given the answer to his prayer.

More important than such aspects of God's answer to his cry for assurance is the word he receives about what constitutes an acceptable sacrifice, as we shall now proceed to see.

The beloved man as an acceptable sacrifice

'*Now therefore, O our God, hearken to the prayer of thy servant . . . and for thy own sake, O Lord, cause thy face to shine upon thy sanctuary, which is desolate*' (verse 17).

As Daniel prayed for forgiveness and assurance, his mind was dwelling on the problem of the interrupted sacrifices at Jerusalem. For centuries it had been believed that the only way the individual or the nation could receive forgiveness and become restored to favour with God was by bringing sacrifices to the temple. The guilty worshipper, after he had committed sin, brought his animal to the altar and laid his hand on its head, confessing his sin and thus transferring the sin to the victim. The animal was slain as a substitute or exchange for the life of the offerer; he was assured by the priest of his forgiveness, and a meal of fellowship with God was eaten.[2] At regular intervals there were services of atonement for the guilt of the whole community when the broken covenant between God and the nation was regarded as being restored through a certain ritual of sacrifice.[3] The sacrifices were instituted to show people that when they came to God for forgiveness, communion and strength there had to be a putting right of sin—an atonement—and that this was a costly and fearful business involving the acceptance of punishment and the full recognition of the infinitely serious consequences of their breach

[1]Is. 43:1.   [2]*Cf.* Lv. 4:27–31; 7:11–15.   [3]Lv. 16.

of God's covenant, and the injury they had done to God's name and honour.

But now for Daniel in Babylon the problem was acute: how could God possibly forgive and restore the nation when no-one was making these sacrifices at the altar in the ruined temple, and there were no services for atonement? He believed God required sacrifice and that sacrifice was right. All he could do in his plea for forgiveness, therefore, was to plead with God to cause his *face to shine upon thy sanctuary, which is desolate* (verse 17) and to remember the sacrifices that had been made in the past, and accept Israel for the sake of these and of the temple and altar still there in ruins. We cannot but believe that it was deliberate and significant that he made his prayer *at the time of the evening sacrifice* (verse 21), in the hope that somehow that very time might have some virtue before God. He pleaded with God to accept him and his prayer because of what he had made this temple and city come to mean. *'O my God, incline thy ear and hear; open thy eyes and behold our desolations, and the city which is called by thy name; for we do not present our supplications before thee on the ground of our righteousness, but on the ground of thy great mercy. O Lord, hear; O Lord, forgive; O Lord, give heed and act; delay not, for thy own sake, O my God, because thy city and thy people are called by thy name'* (verses 18, 19).

But now suddenly the astonishing message is conveyed to him that the old sacrifices are no longer necessary, and that he himself and his prayers are accepted because in them God finds a sacrifice which pleases him better. *'O Daniel, I have now come out to give you wisdom and understanding. At the beginning of your supplications a word went forth, and I have come to tell it to you, for you are greatly beloved'* (verse 23).

The true sacrifice God wants is the sacrifice of the heart. *'You are greatly beloved.'* There was no need for Daniel now to stress the sacrifices of bulls and goats, to plead forgiveness for their absence, to ask God to base his forgiveness on their supposed continuance. God desires faithful covenant love before animal sacrifice. He looks on the heart of the man before him, rather than on the shed blood on the altar and the rising smoke from the censer. Daniel is to be judged, heard, and, with his prayers, accepted or rejected, because of what he offers to God personally in his faith in God's purposes. He is accepted because he believes in God, and in what God is going to do for the future of Israel. This is what God is henceforth going to build his restored Jerusalem upon.

Daniel is rediscovering for himself the message of many of the prophets and psalms that the sacrifice that most pleased God was that of a pure heart and upright life.[1] They must not trust merely in their temple ceremonies, but must right wrongs and relieve the oppressed. It took a long time for this lesson to sink in. Now we know what it all finally means. Daniel's sense of being accepted for the sake of his own faith and his own self-surrender was only a half-way stage towards the understanding of the full truth which had one day to come to God's people. We ourselves through Christ and his sacrifice have learnt that the whole system of sacrifice in the temple at Jerusalem was temporary and shadowy. It merely pointed to a final reality that was one day to be fulfilled in history. It was effective and accepted by God only because it was a pointer to the one *real* offering, the one *real* sacrifice, the one *real* atonement that would be made when the one true High Priest would come to represent all mankind in his person and offer himself to God for the sake of all, in the place of any who henceforth would look to him for forgiveness.

Surely it is much easier for us than even for Daniel to attain this new sense of personal acceptance by God and to know that our prayers too are accepted and heard. We may have no visible angel, but we have Christ who has replaced all sacrifices, who has given us his name to plead, who has delivered us even from the need to wait till our own hearts become pure and our own lives become perfect.[2] If we belong to him we are beloved, and we can ask, confident that we will be heard. If we ask what he wills for us, our prayers are bound to be heard, and what he wills for us will be effected by our asking. 'Whatever you ask in my name, I will do it, that the Father may be glorified in the Son; if you ask anything in my name, I will do it.'[3] 'If you abide in me, and my words abide in you, ask whatever you will, and it shall be done for you.'[4]

The angels and the answer

The answer is brought by the angel called *Gabriel* (verse 21). Sometimes he is called an archangel for he seems to have had an

[1] 1 Sa. 15:22, 23; Is. 1:11–17; Ps. 40:6; Ps. 51:16, 17; Je. 29:12–14.
[2] Heb. 4:14–16; 8:1, 2; 10:19–22.   [3] Jn. 14:13, 14.
[4] Jn. 15:7.

important place among other angels. The book of Daniel now forces us to take note of these creatures as they fly down from another realm in which the Lord is exalted and supreme, conveying his messages and taking part along with us in his services. Since they are mentioned not in our creeds, but rather in our hymns, it is sometimes asserted that they belong only to the periphery of the Christian faith, that their work and service should not be taken too seriously. But if we find ourselves able sincerely to sing about angels, we should be prepared to discuss the matter. A very wise Old Testament scholar once observed that in the matter of angels we had to be on our guard against two extremes—that of a 'vulgar credulity' and that of a 'presumptuous incredulity.'[1]

We are so sceptical today that our first concern must be to avoid the incredulity. Where God is at work in saving us through Christ the angels are also there, not simply rejoicing and wondering,[2] not only giving fellowship and encouragement,[3] but also working and making their own contribution to the achievement of God's will.[4] They seem to be given a special charge in exercising providential care for individuals.[5] Surely then we must try to leave our minds and our hearts as open as we can to what they have to say to us and do for us. Karl Barth reminds us of the text in Hebrews: 'Do not neglect to show hospitality to strangers, for thereby some have entertained angels unawares.'[6] His interpretation[7] suggests that it is the angels themselves who are the strangers, and we ourselves who have to be willing to entertain them in a more central place in our thinking than we have perhaps hitherto given them. We certainly must not be over-credulous or make more fuss of the angels than Scripture itself makes. We cannot invoke angels or seek to commune with them. Nowhere in the Bible are angels asked to take prayers of people up to God, or to act as mediators between human beings and God, though they can make intercession.[8] This passage we are studying is typical of others. Gabriel, the angel sent by God to Daniel, has nothing to do with enabling Daniel to attain communion with God, or to gain the ear of God. Daniel takes no initiative in seeking Gabriel out and he

[1]John Duncan, *Colloquia Peripatetica*[2] (Edinburgh, 1890), p. 39.
[2]Lk. 2:10; 15:10.   [3]Rev. 22:8, 9; Mt. 4:11.
[4]Heb. 1:14; Mt. 24:31; Lk. 1:19.
[5]Ps. 91:11; Mt. 26:53; 2 Ki. 6:16, 17.   [6]Heb. 13:2.
[7]*Church Dogmatics*, 3.3, p. 415.   [8]Zc. 1:12.

does not think of giving him a message. God hears our prayers directly, and Christ is the one mediator between God and man. In his name we pray, and for his sake we are received and heard.

But men are helped to wisdom and understanding by angel messengers. Gabriel brings to Daniel the *word* that *went forth* for Daniel *at the beginning of* his prayer (verse 23), and Gabriel seems to be able to encourage and fortify Daniel[1] and to impart understanding (verse 22). Angels thus seem to have the power to communicate with the human and to inspire and promote thoughts, and they bring with their presence an assurance of being accepted. As we study the book further we find the angels involved in the cosmic conflict between the powers of evil and God himself.

The God of angels and mankind

When Daniel prayed he was not seeking to have any kind of dealings with angels at all; he was seeking God himself. *I turned my face to the Lord God, seeking him* (verse 3). Face to face with God, in the Bible, implies frank and open personal relationship. There is in Daniel's prayer the note of intimate personal pleading that we find in the Psalms: *'Hearken to the prayer of thy servant and to his supplications'* (verse 17).[2]

But suddenly, instead of the immediate presence of God, he finds an angel who speaks as though he had 'come down' from a realm 'up there'. Between himself and the Lord to whom he had hoped to be close, there is now revealed a distance that seems infinite. God appears, at the moment, to have lost the features of the familiar friend and to be distant and too exalted for any possible friendship between him and a mere man.

Yet all the comfort and intimacy he needs are there when the angel brings the message. Daniel, *greatly beloved*, learns that it is the exalted God who is the familiar God, and that the familiar God must always remain the exalted God. He is helped to learn the lesson taught by another of the great prophets: 'I dwell in the high and holy place, and also with him who is of a contrite and humble spirit.'[3]

He may have required to learn that God was more above human affairs than he had thought. We can see as we read the book up to this point that he had always believed in, and knew himself to be

[1]*Cf.* 8:18.　　[2]*Cf. e.g.* Pss. 25; 26; 63; 130.　　[3]Is. 57:15.

dealing with, a God who had majestic features as well as familiar and friendly ones. He could never have forgotten his vision of the Ancient of days on the judgment seat among his assessors; and at the beginning of this very intimate and personal prayer to a God who is sought as one near at hand, Daniel addresses him as *the great and terrible God* (verse 4). But he had always tended to stress God's involvement in human history. For Daniel, up to this point, God had been first of all the Lord of human affairs, of Daniel's affairs, of Israel's affairs, of Babylonian affairs, immersed deeply in the current of human events and interested in every detail. But now Daniel is reminded again for his good that the God he is dealing with is above and beyond, has his own life, his own place, and his own fellowship. His blessedness is not destroyed, nor is his being exhausted, by his immersion in history. His throne is never insecure when earthly empires are tottering. He has his heavens, his angels and archangels and other 'myriads of myriads and thousands of thousands'[1]—this and nothing less is to be the setting and the basis for Daniel's new and deeper experience of assurance about prayer.

Is our God too small?

It is helpful for us, too, to learn this kind of lesson. Our own belief about prayer is determined by our belief about God. But we always tend to set our thoughts about God within a very limited framework, to drag God down to exactly our own level, to rob him of whatever attributes are challenging and exalted, and to make him purely one-sided. We therefore so emphasize the glory of his nearness, his involvement in our affairs, his identification with us in our history that we lose sight entirely of his independence of us, of the sublime aspects of his glory. We like to think of him primarily as a God of friendly love—as *we* understand love! We comfort ourselves that we can appeal to him as one who can be moved with compassion, that we can plead with him as one who listens and understands. All this is true about him. But if our relationship with him is to become ultimately satisfying and lasting, we have to anchor ourselves in his eternal and unchangeable faithfulness and omnipotence, as we root ourselves in his love. While he gives us everything we must remember that he himself is none the poorer for all his giving. He is loving and

[1]Rev. 5:11.

just only within the framework of his own sheer exalted holiness.

Jeremiah found that the other prophets of his time had lost all their reverence and fear of God because they had lost all vision of his holiness and majesty. They were teaching about him only the pleasant ideas that they could dream up in their own dreams. They called him a 'God at hand'. Their gospel was of a new friendly God close to people, concerned to love everyone. They omitted to speak about his holiness or anger or insistence that people should turn from the evil of their doings. Jeremiah called upon both prophets and people to look again at the God they were thinking about so one-sidedly, and for the sake of everything they lived for, to regain the truth about him in its wholeness. 'Am I a God at hand, says the Lord, and not a God afar off? Can a man hide himself in secret places so that I cannot see him? says the Lord.'[1] We too lose not only our reverence and fear but also our assurance when we think of him only as being 'at hand' and not also as being 'afar off'.

Jesus told us when we pray to say, 'Our Father, who art in heaven', and he always tried to anchor our thoughts on himself as our trusted friend who will be with us forever, and never fail in friendship and understanding. But the last view he gave of himself was of his ascension to that very heaven into which Daniel's thoughts were raised by the ministry of the angels.[2]

Seventy weeks of years!

The answer to Daniel's prayer for light on Jeremiah's forecast about the length of the Babylonian captivity is given in the short section at the end of the chapter—the 'prophecy of the seventy weeks'. Jeremiah had said that the captivity of the people was to last for seventy years. From which date was the calculation to be made? Were there any signs that the end of the period was beginning to appear? Could Jeremiah have meant the figure to be taken accurately, or perhaps allegorically? Daniel was intent on searching out this one date. He felt that the time must be fairly near at hand now and that it would be an event of great importance in the work God was going to do in history.

The angel Gabriel came and, in effect, said, 'Seventy years for Jeremiah meant *"seventy weeks of years"*' (verse 24). He began to speak not about the return of Israel from Babylon but about a far

[1] Je. 23:23, 24.   [2] Lk. 24:51; Acts 1:9-11.

163

more distant event. It was a challenge to Daniel to lift his eyes off the happenings of the near future (the liberation of Israel from Babylon), to events much more distant and important which have to do with the time of the *end* of all things. Three times in the short word Gabriel brought to Daniel, he speaks about this *end* (verses 24, 26).

This enlargement of Jeremiah's prophecy by Gabriel did not cancel out Jeremiah's literal prophecy that the exile was to be for seventy years. It actually lasted for more or less that time. All such numbers in Holy Scripture are approximate. But Gabriel's word did give Daniel a needed reminder that God had even then bigger things to think about than the return across the desert and the rebuilding of Jerusalem. Moreover the word came to Daniel that exact numerology in forecasting an event is much less important than the business of whether or not it is going to happen.

When we read this new number, seventy times seven years, as an indication of the time of the great final event, we must remember that this too means merely 'approximately five hundred' ($70 \times 7 = 490$). Peter once asked Jesus how often he had to forgive his brother when he sinned against him—was it to be seven times? Jesus replied no—until seventy times seven.[1] He did not mean by this, literally four hundred and ninety times, but was simply using a current approximate phrase to indicate a big number in this context.

The goal of history

What is to be achieved in the climactic period of the *seventy weeks of years* is described at the very beginning of the prophecy in sixfold terms: '*Seventy weeks of years are decreed concerning your people and your holy city, to finish the transgression, to put an end to sin, and to atone for iniquity, to bring in everlasting righteousness, to seal both vision and prophet, and to anoint a most holy place*' (verse 24).

As we read on through the whole prophecy we will find that the author speaks with considerable, and probably deliberate, ambiguity about the opening date of the period of approximately five hundred years of which this verse describes the climax (*cf.* verse 25). This ambiguity allows us to choose any of four different dates as our starting time for the movement towards this climax,

[1]Mt. 18:21, 22.

the achievement described in the twenty-fourth verse of this chapter, linking it either to what happened when the temple was cleansed and rededicated immediately following the fearful events of the persecution under Antiochus Epiphanes, or to what happened when Christ himself died and rose again.

We must have some patience in examining the view honestly held by many scholars, that all these phrases about the finishing of *transgression* and *sin*, atoning for *iniquity* and bringing in of *everlasting righteousness* referred in the mind of the writer himself to what was accomplished in the temple courts at Jerusalem, when, after the terrible persecution by Antiochus, the Jews won their liberty by the grace of God, the temple was cleansed and rededicated, and its evil purged. We have to acknowledge too that after the clear prophecy of this very event in the previous chapter, Daniel's mind was occupied with such a final week of years. This view of the matter would of course fit well into the theory that the book of Daniel was itself a tract for Maccabean times. But no satisfactory answer seems to be given to the question of why the writer of a Maccabean tract or any contemporary scribe or reporter would use such extraordinary language even in the expression of their wildest joy. We can certainly imagine them so exultant that they would want to heap up superlatives and indulge in poetry. But the language of this great verse seems, rather, a cool and calculated attempt to describe the ultimate consummation of Israel's history in an event of cosmic significance involving a coming Messiah and the destiny of all nations—the same kind of happening as that which great prophets like Micah and Isaiah and Jeremiah had already spoken about in their own varied terms.[1] One wonders how, on such a theory of the passage, the writer could have come to imagine that the sacrifice of Onias their high priest (even assuming that this is what is alluded to in verse 26), the valiant efforts of the Maccabean resistance movement, and the faithfulness of the Hasidim, could really have brought about an event that merits the climactic place in world history which is assigned to it in this prophecy.

We have therefore to ask whether there are any cogent reasons why we should not simply acknowledge that this passage describes much more fittingly what happened through the life, death, and resurrection of Christ. We must remember above all,

[1] Mi. 4:1-7; Is. 9:1-7; 11:1-9; Je. 31:31-34.

that this passage does not belong merely to a single book about whose origins scholars disagree. It belongs to a book incorporated within a whole body of Holy Scripture in which all *vision and prophet* (verse 24) has its seal set on it, not by the suffering of Onias or by the exploits of the Maccabees, but by Jesus Christ. When we look back to this passage in the light of his coming, we are bound to recognize that he alone, and neither Onias nor the Maccabees, could have brought in *everlasting righteousness* as he *put an end to sin* and atoned *for iniquity*. The ordinary Christian cannot possibly read all these phrases without also seriously asking: Does this not refer to what happened during the life and death of Jesus himself? The church has for centuries taken this view, and one notable commentator calls this especially a 'Christ-saturated passage'.

The foreshadowing of events to come

We would again underline our view that the book of Daniel was written with the conviction that within the sphere of salvation history, coming events cast their shadow before. In the shape of earlier and smaller events,[1] we can discern the patterns that are going to be manifested in the final events. Thus, in the lesser preliminary events, God produces beforehand a series of happenings typical of what is ultimately going to come.

We must regard it therefore as possible that the passage can actually have a double reference, a feature we find occurring again and again in Holy Scripture. For example, it seems most likely that in Psalm 22 the writer is describing either his own personal sufferings, or perhaps the collective sufferings of his community, the people of God, as they sought to be true servants of God. But at the same time the Psalm refers also to the sufferings of Christ.[2] In Psalm 16, when the psalmist gave expression to his hope of ultimate resurrection in the ninth and tenth verses—'my body also dwells secure. For thou dost not give me up to Sheol'—he was uttering a personal hope, but at the same time, in some way, 'being ... a prophet ... he foresaw and spoke of the resurrection of the Christ'.[3] Joyce Baldwin says that 'a characteristic of apocalyptic is using past events to typify a supremely important future event'. She finds this characteristic used in Zechariah 9, where the writer suggests that 'just as successive alien armies

---

[1]See above, pp. 144 ff.   [2]*Cf.* Mt. 27:46.   [3]Acts 2:30, 31.

swept through Syria and Palestine and claimed a right to each territory, so finally the Lord will see every proud city capitulate to Him'.[1]

Therefore, when in reading the Bible we come across such examples of what we may even call 'doubletalk'—such descriptions of incidents or references to incidents which seem in the very description to carry more meaning than the incidents immediately referred to could contain—we are justified in believing that it could have been the intention even of the original writer (as well as the Holy Spirit), to refer to something he felt belonged to the fulfilment of the great future purpose of God for Israel and the world. Someone reading the fifty-third chapter of Isaiah might be justified in understanding it first of all as the story of some suffering prophet of God[2] or as the account of Israel's own deepest conscious thought about its own destiny in the service of God. But we would miss its truest meaning if we did not see it also as a prophecy of Jesus. Moreover, when we read the story of Abraham's sacrifice of Isaac in Genesis chapter 22, it would be short-sighted indeed if we failed to see the deepest levels of meaning that this chapter contains as a prophecy both of Israel's future and of Christ's sacrifice, because we were so taken up with what it meant subjectively as a crowning incident of Abraham's life.

Therefore, as we face this verse before us, our minds here spring up in faith, and we think of Jesus. He, indeed, is the one who has come to 'put an end to sin',[3] the havoc it works in our minds and hearts,[4] the inhumanity it brings to our dealings with each other, and the darkness and uncertainty in which it shrouds the meaning and destiny of our lives.[5] He, indeed, has come to lift the burden and cancel the bondage of our past,[6] to 'atone for iniquity' and to open up a way for us to come back to our heavenly Father and to be welcomed again into the heart of his love.[7] He and he alone has died to establish everywhere, and to bring each of us personally as his gift, an 'everlasting righteousness'[8] which means for us here and now great new possibilities for integrity, openness, and trustworthiness in our own personal lives, and also the deliverance and vindication of the oppressed and the

[1]*Haggai, Zechariah Malachi* (Tyndale Old Testament Commentary, Inter-Varsity Press, 1972), p. 158.

[2]*Cf.* Acts 8:34.   [3]Mt. 1:21; Jn. 19:30; Heb. 9:26.   [4]Jn. 8:34-36.
[5]Heb. 2:14, 15.   [6]Col. 2:13-15.   [7]Lk. 15:20; Eph. 1:7.
[8]Rom. 3:21-26; Acts 17:30, 31.

establishment of a just social order.[1] He it is who spoke of the temple of his own body as the 'most holy place'[2] which would bear the final and effective 'anointing',[3] when as the true high priest he would offer himself, through the eternal Spirit, without spot, to God, in place of all the old and now ineffectual blood-sacrifices.[4]

The working out of the purpose of God

Gabriel told Daniel that the history of the people of God within the 490-year span (seventy weeks of years) was to develop in three distinct phases: one of *seven weeks* (verse 25a, forty-nine years), one of *sixty-two weeks* (verse 25b, 434 years), and one of *one week* (verse 27, seven years).

At the beginning of the first period there is to be the *going forth of the word to restore and build Jerusalem*. This event could be the oracle uttered by Jeremiah in Jeremiah 25:11, which could be dated 605 BC. It could also be the oracle uttered by the same prophet in Jeremiah 29:10, which could be dated 598 BC. Since this decree became effective in history when Jerusalem was destroyed in 587 BC, some have taken this last figure as the effective starting-date. But the same *going forth of the word to restore and rebuild* could also refer to the permission given by Cyrus to the exiles to return to Palestine in 538 BC, or it could refer to the decree of Artaxerxes I in 458 BC, mentioned in the book of Ezra.[5]

The *coming of an anointed one* (verse 25) at the end of this first period has to be interpreted by some event we can place approximately forty-nine years after our opening event. Those who want the climactic week to fall in the time of Antiochus, *c.* 150 BC, take an early date, and it is possible to regard the anointed one as Cyrus, the Persian king,[6] or as Zerubbabel, the princely descendant of the Davidic line referred to especially in Zechariah,[7] or to Joshua, the high priest associated with Zerubbabel.[8] Cyrus made his significant appearance in history in 539 BC. Zerubbabel and Joshua did their work round about 520 BC. If we choose 458 BC as a starting point, on the other hand (so as to reach the time of Christ at the end of the whole period), we must suppose that some other event corresponded to the 'coming of an anointed one.'

[1] 2 Pet. 1:3–8; Lk. 4:18.   [2] Jn. 2:19–22.   [3] Lk. 3:22; Mk. 14:8, 9.
[4] Heb. 9:6, 7, 12, 13.   [5] Ezr. 7:11 ff.   [6] *Cf.* Is. 45:1 ff.
[7] Zc. 4:6 ff.; *cf.* Ezr. 2:2.   [8] *I.e.* Zc. 3; 6:9 ff.

Then the second period follows—a very lengthy one of *sixty-two weeks* of years in which nothing worth mentioning is seen to happen at all. But since this long period is immediately followed by the critical final week of years (NEB, *the critical time*), we know that during it there has been a very deep, though underground, development of attitudes, circumstances, personalities and traditions all working together to produce the final critical phase. It is a period in which the pressure is allowed to mount up for the final climax, final conflict, final decision—for even in this history (as in all history) nothing is really final or decisive till the outcome of this final week.

When we now turn to look at this last 'week of years', we find it begins, *An anointed one will be cut off* (verse 26). Those who regard the prophecy as being strictly messianic, *i.e.* referring to Christ alone, hear this as a direct reference to the events of his death on the cross. The following reference to the *strong covenant* and the cessation of *sacrifice* (verse 27) is therefore to the new covenant and the abolition of the validity of the old sacrifices. The reference to the destruction of the sanctuary is to the destruction of Jerusalem under Titus when the temple was again desecrated. The *wing* on which the *abominations* were set up can refer to the pinnacle of the temple, or the ramp which led to the altar.

Those who regard the passage as containing either a prophecy or a description of the events that took place in Jerusalem under Antiochus Epiphanes interpret the *anointed one* who was *cut off* as referring either to the removal (in 175 BC) or to the murder (in 170 BC) of Onias, the high priest, who was supplanted by favourites of Antiochus—Jason and Menelaus. The destruction of the city and sanctuary by *the people of the prince* (verse 26) can refer to the pillaging of Jerusalem in 168 BC by mercenary troops. The *strong covenant with many* is a reference to the support given to Antiochus by many apostate Jews. The cessation of *sacrifice and offering* and the desolating sin refer to Antiochus' final attempt to destroy Jewish religion by decreeing that there should be no sacrifices, and that an altar dedicated to Zeus should be set up in the sanctuary. The decree of Antiochus caused the offerings to be suspended for a period of about three years, from December 167 to December 164.

When we consider how we are to fit into one of these beginnings and one of these endings our intervening period of sixty-two weeks of years, *i.e.* approximately 434 years, we find ourselves in difficulties as great as those of deciding at what period to begin and when to end. Those who favour the earlier date for the final week of years have difficulty. If we take the issuing of the decree to be one of the earliest dates, and the coming of the anointed one to be Cyrus in 538 BC, then the difference between this date and 170 BC is only 368 years. Those who support this view say that the difference is due to an error in the current chronology used by the Jews at the time the book of Daniel was written. If we take a date round about that of the death of Jesus as the final date, then we also have difficulties, but they are fewer in this matter than are confronted by the other view. It is to be noted that even many conservative expositors find this such a difficult prophecy that they tend to regard the numbers as more symbolic than accurate.

In deciding about this very controversial passage we must not imagine that our whole understanding of what the book of Daniel has to say to us today depends on our getting this interpretation absolutely right. What we decide here affects our interpretation of only a section of a book of the Bible which on every account is great. Perhaps the whole prophecy is meant deliberately to be vague and enigmatic. It is not for us to know exact dates too confidently. The end can come at any time, and we must be on the watch always, for signs of the times change around us.

Daniel 10
'I Daniel'

The final encounter

THIS chapter tells how Daniel received a vision or 'word' which somehow conveyed to him that there lay some time in the future a period of intense suffering and trial that might involve him in some hard task (verses 1 and 10). It was to be the final word he would receive about what was to happen in the future. When it came, he was prepared to receive it, for he had been overcome by an unusually deep sense of his own sin and that of his community. *For three weeks*, in order to give himself to prayer, he had abstained from anything more than the barest necessity in the way of food (verses 2, 3). His period of fasting included the week of the passover during which the people of Israel were reminded of the 'bread of affliction' which they had to eat as they were delivered from bondage in Egypt as a reminder of their bitter sufferings in that land.[1] Perhaps also he went into retreat with some friends (*cf.* verse 7), for the vision he had prepared for came to him when he was *on the bank of the great river, that is the Tigris* (verse 4).

There something suddenly seems to have happened that was more than a mere dream or an ordinary 'vision'. When Paul was converted on the Damascus Road,[2] the Christ who stood before him and spoke was there present to him, not simply as a vision private to the mind of one individual, and only within the mind of one individual. Strangely and marvelously, he was there as he had been to his disciples in the upper room, the man who had been slain come back from the tomb, risen, heavenly, but no less real and 'objective' than he had been when he was with them in the

[1]Dt. 16:3; Ex. 12.   [2]Acts 9:1–9.

flesh.[1] Paul insists on this constantly in all his accounts of his experience,[2] and in the first account of his conversion Acts records that others were with him, too, and heard the voice that came to him although they saw no-one.[3] As Daniel tells us here what happened on the banks of the Tigris, he insists no less strongly that the angel he saw this time was no mere picture in his own mind, for the very sounding of his voice had a remarkable physical effect on the men that were there with him, since *a great trembling fell upon them, and they fled to hide themselves* (verse 7). Daniel himself was more profoundly affected at the moment of the experience, in this particular encounter, than in any of his previous visions. His very appearance became pitiful and abject as if under some physical seizure, and he fell to the ground helpless and passed into *a deep sleep* (verses 8, 9). But the shining, heavenly being *touched* him, wakened him, still *trembling*, and called him to stand on his feet, assuring him that he was a *man greatly beloved*. The one who touched him further assured him that from the moment he had begun his period of fasting and prayer, the heart of God had been moved toward him with a special measure of trust and favour. This heavenly visit by one of such importance and dignity was the result of his openness and prayer.

But even after he had received the encouraging message, Daniel collapsed again (verse 15), all his strength drained from him (verse 17). Another heavenly being, this time *one in the likeness of the sons of men*, came and helped him on the way to recovery (verses 16, 18). We have to notice that at some point in his experience of the presence of this glorious and dazzling figure, Daniel is conscious that other attendants are there, in some way conveying the message this one has to speak and the gracious ministry he has to give to him, acting as his hands, and speaking in his presence with his full authority. Obviously the account is confused, for Daniel was not fully able to distinguish whether it was the hand of the ministering angel or the hand of the divine figure that upheld him (verses 10, 16), or whether it was the voice of the heavenly visitor or the voice of an angel that spoke to him (verses 11, 14). It is only when the narrative reaches verse 20 that it becomes clear that the figure has disappeared and only an angel remains. This is the one who claimed to be a fellow angel along with Michael, the guardian angel of the people of God,

[1]*Cf.* Lk. 24:28–31.　　[2]*E.g.* 1 Cor. 15:3–8.　　[3]Acts 9:7

concerned to maintain the victory of the people of God in the heavenly realm, as Daniel himself was, in the earthly realm, and ready to speak to Daniel in detail about the future of his people.

The shattering and exalting presence

'*I lifted up my eyes and looked, and behold, a man clothed in linen, whose loins were girded with gold of Uphaz. His body was like beryl, his face like the appearance of lightning, his eyes like flaming torches, his arms and legs like the gleam of burnished bronze, and the sound of his words like the noise of a multitude*' (verses 5, 6).

Daniel's previous experiences of angels and visions had disturbed him greatly, but this one was humbling and shattering to him both physically and emotionally to an unusual degree. And yet, he came out of it in the end, revived, strong, and at peace. The full nature of the experience is well brought out in the translation given in the New English Bible: '*My strength left me; I became a sorry figure of a man, and retained no strength . . . While he spoke to me I hung my head and was struck dumb. Suddenly one like a man touched my lips. Then I opened my mouth to speak . . . "Sir, this has pierced me to the heart, and I retain no strength. How can my lord's servant presume to talk with such as my lord, since my strength has failed me and no breath is left in me?"*' (verses 8, 15–17). But the power to restore and comfort is equally stressed: '*Then the figure touched me again and restored my strength. He said, "Do not be afraid, man greatly beloved; all will be well with you. Be strong, be strong." When he had spoken to me, I recovered strength*' (verses 18, 19).

The exact identity of this figure is left vague. He uses the same manner of approach, the same kind of words, and exercises the same ministry as the angel Gabriel. Yet, throughout the Bible, it is the presence of God alone which produces such humbling and shattering experience, and it is God alone who can comfort and strengthen in such a way. The prophets had this kind of experience when they were in the presence of God himself.[1]

Moreover the same kind of utterly humbling and yet renewing encounter with another person came to the apostles occasionally in the presence of Christ himself. In the first chapter of the book of Revelation there is a description of the appearance of the

[1] Is. 6:4–8; Je. 1:6–10; Ezk. 2:1, 2.

exalted Christ to John on the island of Patmos. In this, Christ assumes the same form as this angelic visitor to Daniel. Both have a shining appearance, bronzed limbs and a belt of gold.[1] Commentators have often assumed that this appearance to Daniel was therefore an appearance of Christ himself.

This interpretation assumes that before Christ came in the flesh in New Testament times, he was there also in Old Testament times, working amongst the people of God who were equally his people, guiding them, bringing them forgiveness, granting them faith and repentance, appealing to them and chastising them just as he did in the Gospel story, and just as he does in the church today. The only difference is that then he was not in the flesh, and what he did was not so vivid and powerful and visible as it was in New Testament times. But it was and is all the same thing—then in an older, passing form, now in a new, continuing and better form. We affirm this when we speak of the continuity of the New Testament with the Old Testament, and interpret the Old Testament people as being already the church, already in living communion with the head of the church. We affirm this, too, when we sing the Old Testament Psalms and, as we sing them, put all our Christian meaning into them, believing that even when they were composed and sung in Old Testament times they had exactly this kind of meaning. Jesus himself encouraged this interpretation of the Old Testament, asserting that before Abraham was called into Ur of the Chaldees he was there, and that Abraham rejoiced to see him.[2]

The climax of all Daniel's experiences, then, comes at the end of his book, just as in the book of Job the climactic vision of seeing God with his own eyes came at the end of this book.[3] Daniel had been moving towards this, and indeed, growing towards it. In this order of events he is different from some of the prophets. Isaiah and Jeremiah, for instance, had dramatic encounters with God, interrupting their lives early in their careers and binding them afterwards to the service of God.[4] They were rather like the man Jesus spoke about, who suddenly and unexpectedly came across 'treasure hidden in a field', thus entering the kingdom through a once-for-all inaugural experience of its glory and power.[5] Daniel was more like the man who collected 'fine pearls',[6] and it was only after a considerable series of finds, one better than another, that

[1]Rev. 1:13–16.   [2]Jn. 8:56–58.   [3]Jb. 38:1—42:6.
[4]Is. 6:1 ff.; Je. 1:1 ff.   [5]Mt. 7:44.   [6]Mt. 13:45, 46.

he found himself ultimately with the 'final thing'.

The cost of involvement and the gift of understanding

It is remarkable that at this point in his career, when the word of God seemed to come in a personal way closer to him than ever before, and pressed its claim upon his life and loyalty most intensely, Daniel should have required so much help to come to grips with what was being demanded of him, and should have found the task of understanding the message such a toil. He was obviously in great agony of mind and heart as he received and pondered what was communicated. The New English Bible accurately reflects the whole drift of the chapter in its translation of the first verse: *Though this word was true, it cost him much toil to understand it; nevertheless understanding came in the course of the vision.* Somehow the drift of what was being said was not obvious. *The sound of his words* was *like the noise of a multitude* (verse 6). At first, under the impact of the vision and the speaking, his mind was powerfully overcome by a kind of sleepy stupor (verse 9), and he had to labour to come to comprehension, and to make himself face up to the implications of the truth of the word.

The vision before him seemed to call for the surrender of all his will and equally of all his mind. There could be no dispute at this moment with the one who stood there before him, no drawing of the line before the pressure of the grace that was seeking to invade his being, no holding back from the total demand on his strength and soul. His life was now about to be taken up afresh into a service that he felt to be dreadful as well as glorious. Can we wonder that he trembled as he yielded?

The cost of close involvement with God and his Word is, of course, brought out vividly in the call of Moses at the burning bush.[1] He raised objection after objection[2] to his attempting the task, revealing how well he knew there and then at the beginning the suffering and toil and risk in which he was to become involved if he responded. And the reality of the suffering he shrank from is brought out to the full in his experiences with his people after they lapsed into their orgies around the golden calf. Relief came when in protest he smashed the tablets of stone against the rocks, but he was forced to go and write them again, and he soon found

[1]Ex. 3:2 ff.   [2]Ex. 3:11 ff.; 4:1 ff., 10 ff.

himself involved in a long protracted agony of praying to God for the forgiveness and restoration of a people whom he himself could hardly bear to live with.[1] The same shrinking before inevitable involvement is expressed, too, unforgettably by Jeremiah:

> O Lord, thou hast deceived me,
>   and I was deceived;
> thou art stronger than I,
>   and thou hast prevailed.
> I have become a laughingstock all the day;
>   every one mocks me.
> For whenever I speak, I cry out,
>   I shout, 'Violence and destruction!'
> For the word of the Lord has become for me
>   a reproach and derision all day long.
> If I say, 'I will not mention him,
>   or speak any more in his name,'
> there is in my heart as it were a burning fire
>   shut up in my bones,
> and I am weary with holding it in,
>   and I cannot.[2]

Both Moses and Jeremiah, as they yielded, found themselves borne along, strangely free, strong, confident, and even joyful, and were sustained to the very end of their lives by the majestic power and love that had at first so overwhelmed them.[3] And with Daniel, too, liberty and light and joy were given to him in the very moment of his commitment. We have already mentioned the significant verses in the passage (verses 10, 16, 18) which tell us how he was awakened and raised to his feet by a gentle angelic touch, how his dumbness was cured and his lips were opened by the same heavenly ministry, and the very one who had brought him such fear, and whose splendour had so blinded him, announced, as it were, with his own voice that he had come indeed to answer his prayer for understanding of the mystery before him.

---

[1]Ex. 32–34. [2]Je. 20:7–9.
[3]*Cf. e.g.* Ex. 34:1–8, 29–35; Je. 15:16; 16:19; 20:11.

The cost must be the same today

The purpose of this detailed account of how Daniel responded to the word of God is not simply to provide us with interesting insight into the unique workings of a prophetic mind, but also to remind us of what it can cost us today to understand, receive, and live with the same kind of 'word'. It is only too easy for us, especially when faced by a book like Daniel, to play the traditional part of a 'student of prophecy', living on in our ease and luxury while we discuss where and how the next beast will arise on the scene of history; how soon and where the battle of Armageddon will take place (a battle in which the horses are to swim in blood!)—and the only agony it costs us is the agony of a little superficial research into strange numbers, and a few not very complicated arithmetical sums.

We will discuss in the next section the further unique significance of the three weeks' fasting in Daniel's ministry, but at present we can note that his 'toil' to understand and receive the word fruitfully did actually involve what we can only call hard labour, self-denial and prayer. In Old Testament times people took seriously the idea that physical fasting helped them as they sought to receive revelation and guidance from God.[1] If we are going to give the problem of interpreting the Bible the concentration it demands, we may be constrained simply to drop a lot of things that otherwise would divert us hopelessly away from our task. Though understanding the Bible is to some extent a gift, there is as much sheer hard labour to be faced in overcoming human difficulties in the course of this understanding as in facing any other ancient text, or as in any other problem of research. We have to be scholars as much as possible. It may be that we can even learn the biblical languages for ourselves, or read up from others the linguistic problems, and work at making our own judgment. The same holds true in understanding the thought forms and literary forms of these past days.

But as ordinary people, without such specialist knowledge, and with the help of good translations, if we can make the Bible the chief book in our lives, so that it is allowed to dominate and mould our thinking as no other book; if we too can take the trouble to read it at the cost of time and to so familiarize ourselves with its great passages so that we are able to repeat many of them from

[1] *Cf.* Ezr. 8:21.

memory; if we too can determine to come to know something of the contours and views of the wide-ranging and fascinating country into which its many books and chapters lead us, then as we do this we shall begin to grasp something of its unity and wholeness and we shall begin to find ourselves able to understand 'difficult' passages and texts by comparing them with other passages and texts that have a clearer meaning. We shall find, as we do all this with sincere and true faith, that the Bible gives itself to us in an extraordinary way. As we keep on seeking, we find, as we keep on knocking, it is opened to us.[1] The door may seem to have lain closed for a long time as we stood there seeking entrance, but eventually our free reward is that new avenues of meaning and enrichment are there indeed, open before us. Moreover we can find ourselves, as Daniel was, helped to fresh understanding if we study the book with others alongside us, or with good expositors and pastors as our heavenly-sent guides.

Notice that while Daniel was struggling to understand, he *humbled* himself before his God (verse 12). He felt that truth could be received only by one surrendered in heart to the giver of the revelation, and willing to accept all the practical implications of knowing it and of being obedient to it. Such utter humility before the truth does not only imply that we are willing to brace ourselves to carry out its practical precepts or implications, but also that we are willing so deeply and fully to submit our understanding and thinking to the truth, that we allow it to shape our very minds themselves. We have to let the word dictate the way our thoughts have to go, the paths they have to follow, as we respond mentally. We have to yield up our self-will in the movement of our own minds, as we submit ourselves to the truth before us, and thus to the God who himself is before us in this truth. It was this kind of response John Calvin was thinking of when he said that 'a true knowledge of God is born out of obedience'.[2]

The communion of heaven and earth in the cosmic conflict

Towards the end of the chapter a remarkable revelation is given to Daniel of how both angels and human beings are involved deeply in one and the same conflict, and fight alongside each other exactly the same enemies. Moreover, the heavenly host in their

[1]*Cf.* Pr. 2:1-11; Lk. 11:9 ff.   [2]*Institutes*, 1.6.2.

conflict need the support of earthly intercessors, and the earthly people of God in their conflict have the help of the heavenly host. We are indeed given a remarkable revelation of the communion of heaven and earth in the cosmic conflict.

In addition to being messengers, the angels are patrons and guardians of communities and nations and possibly of individuals on earth. We have already seen Gabriel with his special concern for Daniel. We have also noticed the 'watchers' who are concerned with the discipline and welfare of Nebuchadnezzar.[1] Michael seems to have guardianship over Israel as a nation. Among others there is one called *the prince of Persia*, another *the prince of Greece* (verse 20). In their midst there is this especially important one who introduces himself to Daniel in this chapter and who seems to be higher than any other.

The most important aspect of this revelation is that the conflicts and tensions between earthly powers and the people of God are reflected in the heavenly realm, and are also being fought out there. A tension between Persia and the people of God is reflected in a conflict between *the prince of the kingdom of Persia* and Michael (verse 13). The coming threat to the people of God by the Greek empire is reflected in an approaching heavenly conflict between Michael and *the prince of Greece* (verses 20, 21). Even more remarkable is the fact that Daniel's most intense agony, when he fasted and prayed with great conflict of soul, took place during the period of a great struggle in heaven between Michael and the prince of Persia (verses 3, 12). The conflict ended in victory for Michael, but the implication is that Daniel himself, in his sensitivity to what was going on in the other realm, was caught up into this conflict, was able to participate in it through his prayers, and thus to help to bring about sooner the successful outcome. So grateful were the heavenly powers for the help of Daniel's prayers that the heavenly messenger came to thank him and strengthen him in the weakness the conflict had caused him, and to encourage him to go on praying with the same concern and anxiety. '*Do you know why I have come to you? But now I will return to fight against the prince of Persia; and when I am through with him, lo, the prince of Greece will come*' (verse 20). It is as if he wanted Daniel to enter a solemn pact to continue praying while the heavenly conflict lasted, because he had no other support: '*There is none who contends by my side against*

[1]4:13.

these except Michael, your prince' (verse 21).

It is thus asserted that in the heavenly sphere there is some kind of participation in the conflicts and troubles of earth; and in the earthly sphere, especially through the intercession of the people of God, there can be some kind of participation in working out of destiny on a much more cosmic scale than is often understood.

We have to make an important choice in evaluating this remarkable elaboration of the function of angels, and of the interaction between the heavenly and earthly spheres. Some scholars warn us that the elaboration of the doctrine of angels was a feature of later Jewish writing when perhaps the thought of God became more remote and prophecy was ceasing, and many strange ideas that were not healthy developments of the great biblical doctrines were taking shape in the mind of Judaism. But before we dismiss all this as a purely peripheral development in biblical teaching, we ought to recall that the New Testament itself not only accepts this elaboration of the doctrine of angels, but gives it a place in its understanding of the work that Christ came to do in the atonement, and also uses it to reinforce its warnings and exhortations to us about the conflict in which we are engaged as we live the Christian life,[1].

The decisive heavenly war

The concept of a heavenly conflict which deeply affects, and is affected by, what takes place on earth, is taken up in the twelfth chapter of the book of Revelation (which, as we have already pointed out, is dependent on Daniel). 'Now war arose in heaven, Michael and his angels fighting against the dragon; and the dragon and his angels fought, but they were defeated and there was no longer any place for them in heaven.'[2] This decisive heavenly war is regarded by the writer of the book of Revelation as taking place in the heavenly sphere at the precise time when Jesus himself in his death and resurrection was engaging and defeating all the powers of evil in the earthly arena. John in his vision sees the war in heaven ending triumphantly just at the time when Jesus finishes his work on the cross and commits himself and the world into the Father's hands. In triumph at that moment, 'the great dragon was thrown down, that ancient serpent, who is called the Devil and Satan, the deceiver of the whole world—he

[1]*Cf. e.g.* Eph. 3:10; 6:10–12.   [2]Rev. 12:7, 8.

was thrown down to the earth, and his angels were thrown down with him'.[1] The thought is that Jesus, through his atoning work on the cross, has brought about a cleansing and reconciliation in heavenly places as well as a reconciliation between God and man on earth. His death has brought decisive victory over all the powers of evil everywhere. This is what he came to achieve and what he rejoiced in beforehand, when, on hearing of the preliminary success of his disciples, he said, 'I saw Satan fall like lightning from heaven.'[2]

This particular vision in the book of Revelation ends with the devil on his way to the bottomless pit, being cast down to earth as a broken power, but still able to harass and hinder the work of God and the people of God for a season.[3] Till the second coming and final triumph of Christ we will therefore wrestle on earth against what Paul calls 'the principalities, ... the powers, ... the spiritual hosts of wickedness in the heavenly places'.[4] It is significant that for victory in this struggle, besides using the armour of truth, righteousness, and faith in the Word, Paul tells us we must 'pray at all times in the Spirit, with all prayer and supplication'.[5]

[1]Rev. 12:9.   [2]Lk. 10:18.   [3]Rev. 12:12.   [4]Eph. 6:12.
[5]Eph. 6:18.

Daniel 11

The history inscribed in the book

Take-over by the spoken word

THIS chapter introduces a spoken apocalypse rather than a visionary one. The essence of what is communicated is given in a long verbal narrative. The form of communication, like that of the prophecy of the seventy weeks, contrasts remarkably with that used in the former revelations to Daniel in chapters 7 or 8. It contrasts also with the dream form of revelation used in the case of Nebuchadnezzar. In those previous visions and dreams the message given was first portrayed in visible dramatic pictures. Afterwards its meaning was clarified by an explanation of the symbols. But here in the last revelation the whole matter is simply narrated in words, sometimes difficult to interpret but often so clear and precise as to make the meaning definite, and there are no visual illustrations. It is a revelation to the ear rather than to the eye. We must assume that since this is the climax of the 'revelations' made to Daniel, this change of focus from the visual to the auditory experience is made so that Daniel and his readers themselves may attain greater clarity and certainty about the message they receive.

Throughout the Bible as a whole, God in his communications to man uses visible symbols as well as words. But it is noticeable that even in most visions these visible elements are never so important as the words that explain them. God takes hold of men and women far more often by an auditive rather than by a visual approach. And even when he uses audio-visual method, the 'audio' always seems to have priority over the 'visual'.

It is a pity that we ourselves too often attempt to reverse the balance of this approach in our efforts to make God and the Christian faith relevant today. We do this in the belief that

182

modern man's mind is conditioned largely by television, and is more receptive to what is seen rather than to what is spoken. But the central question to be faced when we are determining our policy is whether God himself has decided to change his own policy in the means he wills to use. It is foolish of us too lightly to assume that seeing does now have precedence to hearing. We need to have second thoughts today about the importance of words. They are far less ambiguous and far more penetrating and flexible for dynamic use than visual symbols. It is true that even in verbal communication there still remains a measure of ambiguity. What words mean to one person is sometimes very different from what they mean to another. Yet words have the greatest fixity of meaning. And words can be used in a speech with remarkable force and clarity, definiteness and urgency. But the gulf between what the same visual image means to one person and what it means to another is far greater than that between what the same word means. In spite of the most skilful use of technique and artistry in one of our modern, visually conveyed messages, there is seldom the clarity or definiteness of meaning that is necessary when matters of life and death, salvation or judgment are urgently at stake.

The history of the broken empire and its issue

This chapter, throughout its first thirty-five verses at least, re-tells the history of the period we already briefly reviewed in vision in chapter 8 as we watched the exploits of the ram, the he-goat, the four horns, and the little horn. At the beginning of the recapitulation we are given only a few more historical details than we had before. For instance in verse 2 we are told that there were three Persian emperors who finally gave way to one greater than them all who engaged in a costly war against Greece. Commentators find it difficult to define exactly who all these are, but most think that it is the campaign of the great Xerxes that is finally referred to. In verse 3 we are undoubtedly told again about Alexander the Great. The fourth verse tells us what happened at his death: four kingdoms first arose (the four horns of 8:8). 'Cassander obtained Macedonia and Greece, Lysimachus, Thrace and Bithynia, Seleucus Syria, Babylonia and other Eastern countries as far as the Indus, while Ptolemy remained in

183

possession of Egypt.'[1] The fifth verse tells us a little of how the already mentioned Seleucus rose to his kingdom and power, beginning under the protection of Ptolemy in Egypt but gradually moving on to strength and independence towards the north. The date has now moved to about 300 BC.

After we ourselves move to verse 6, the story is dominated for a long time by a series of interactions, alliances and wars between the kings of the north and the kings of the south. The kings of the south are the Ptolemaic kings of Egypt. The kings of the north are the Seleucid kings of the region round about Syria and Palestine, whose capital city was Antioch, and who sometimes took the name Antiochus. The events mentioned in verse 6 took place round about 250 BC. In an attempt to make peace and unite the two kingdoms, Ptolemy II gave his daughter Berenice in marriage to Antiochus II. As we read the verse we are meant to think of this young princess, made a pawn in a political game, arriving in splendour and gaiety at the foreign palace, but soon to find herself the object of a ruthless family conspiracy, and ultimately to be murdered with her offspring by Seleucus II, her stepson, on the instigation of his divorced and jealous mother.

Verses 7–9 tell of the war between Ptolemy III and Seleucus II which arose in the aftermath of this murder. Ptolemy, from the south, ravages and plunders the northern territories. But Seleucus manages to make a partial recovery for an unsuccessful invasion of Egypt. By the end of verse 9, the date is approximately 240 BC.

From verses 10–12 the two main contestants are now Ptolemy III and Antiochus III, who later earned the title Antiochus the Great. He is included in verse 10 simply as one of the two *sons* of the king of the north who take the war to the *fortress* of the south. But his brother, Seleucus III, was murdered while this expedition was in progress and he, Antiochus, was left as the sole Seleucid ruler. The result of this expedition, however, was (verse 11) a strong reaction from Ptolemy III, who defeated his northern opponent in the great battle of Raphia in 205 BC. This battle was followed by a time of peace in which Antiochus was able gradually to recover his strength, and verse 13 opens with the account of the elaborately prepared and successful attempt he launched against Egypt, now ruled by Ptolemy IV. Verse 14 mentions that Antiochus attracted allies (one of them was Philip of Macedonia). It mentions, too, some *men of violence* among the Jews as taking

[1] S. R. Driver, *The Book of Daniel* (The Cambridge Bible, 1900), p. 115.

part on his side in some unsuccessful attempt to *fulfil* a *vision*. No commentator seems to be able to give any likely guess as to what this means.

Verses 15 and 16 tell of the protracted and complicated struggle between Antiochus and Ptolemy IV, ending about 198 BC with the complete ascendency of the former over *the glorious land* (no doubt Palestine) which brought about the ultimately fateful domination of the Jewish people by the Seleucid dynasty. Verse 17 speaks of a further campaign by Antiochus the Great to the south. This ended in the marriage of his daughter Cleopatra to the reigning Ptolemy in 194 BC. She thus won a huge dowry, from which her father no doubt expected to benefit, but finally she proved herself independent.

Verses 18 and 19 describe the last episode in the career of Antiochus the Great. He made an expedition to the west, but came to a disastrous end when in retreat he tried to rob a heathen temple and was killed.

Verse 20 describes the career of Seleucus IV. He was undistinguished and he too, had an ignoble end. But he was certainly better than the younger brother who followed him on the throne—the *contemptible person*, the ignoble Antiochus Epiphanes with whom we have grown so familiar.[1]

Now, from verse 21 on, we read more of the details of his career. Up till this time we have been told little about the thinking and feelings of the people who have taken part in the working out of this history, but now, in his case, we are given a glimpse into his inner aims and motives. He is introduced with a general assessment of his character, in which the treachery and intrigue by which he came to power are stressed (verses 21–24). Then his first Egyptian campaign of 170–169 BC is described, and again his expertness in underhand work is emphasized (verse 25–28). Then there is a glance at a second Egyptian campaign from which he had to withdraw. It is suggested that his rage over this made him turn against the Jews (verse 29, 30a). Then comes the old story of his alliance with the apostate among the Jews, his fierce persecution of those who dared to keep God's convenant, the desecration of temple and altar.

The description in verse 33 of the resistance put up by the faithful Jews, *the people who know their God* (verse 32), is worth special study. *Those among the people who are wise shall make*

---

[1] See above, pp. 139 f., 144 ff.

many understand (verse 33). This could refer to the Hasidim party,[1] or simply to those of the faithful who could see through what was taking place and were prepared in mind to resist false compromising leadership. Their stand and witness had a very great influence in stirring up public opinion and in creating a resistance party even though such politics involved them in a period of martyrdom for civil disobedience. The description of the *little help* (verse 34) which this persecuted group received in their agony may refer to the work of the Maccabees with their policy of armed resistance. It is noticeable that alongside the mention of such allies we have the reminder that even at such a time as this, mingling with such freedom fighters were those who *join themselves to them with flattery* (verse 34), having insincere motives even as they skirted martyrdom in their external allegiance to what seemed to be a course likely now to triumph in the end. This part of the story ends with a triumphant note of consolation for those who have actually been martyred for the cause, and who no doubt themselves died even with hope, for they are cleansed and made *white until the time of the end* (verse 35).

God shapes the pattern of our ways

This passage, read simply within the narrative as we have it, claims to be history told beforehand in fairly well defined detail. As we have seen, often the kings referred to can be named, and the incidents delineated can be traced to actual happenings. It is unusual in the Bible for distant history to be foretold so accurately in such lengthy catalogues and with such minute details. The great prophets undoubtedly foretold at times what God was going to do in the future but they did not go into such a persistent description of minutiae and, on the whole, left many of the circumstances of their predictions vague.

If we are to take the Bible seriously as a whole, we must maintain the view that God is the God of the individual as well as of communities, and that he controls history in such a way as to give free play to human decision, and opportunity for genuine human repentance. He makes room for his own answers to prayers for help, and deliverance, change in circumstances, and the coming of his kingdom. While he rules, he also wills that we should will to avoid the fearful tragedies that we sometimes fall

[1]See above, pp. 15 f.

into as a result of our wilful behaviour. It is as one who gives place to such freedom that he over-rules and orders the affairs of history and accomplishes his purposes. For instance, if we read the story of David and his family fortunes in the aftermath of his sin with Bathsheba, as it is all described in 2 Samuel and in the beginning of 1 Kings, we will find ourselves spectators of a human story marked as much by lust, murder, rape, incest, fratricide, treason, cruelty and neglect as that of the rise and passing of the Seleucid and Ptolemaic dynasties. We know that in this history God is working out his purpose, furthering his will, ensuring that David's son Solomon and no other will succeed him. Yet God makes very little, if any, direct or dramatic intervention in order to give any superhuman twist to affairs. Each human agent whose action determines the shape of history is in his hands and makes free and responsible decisions before him. Prayers, too, are heard and answered. Yet, at the same time, so firmly does God himself shape the events that occur that the grim and precisely detailed prophecy of Absalom's violation of his father's concubines on the roof of David's palace is given long before it occurs.[1] We can think of how, in much the same way—exercising complete sovereignty and yet at the same time leaving room for free human decision—God worked his will in (for example) the story of Joseph and his brothers,[2] and in the crucifixion of Jesus.[3]

We have our responsibility

If we believe, therefore, that the account of the Seleucids and Ptolemies in our present chapter is a predictive prophecy, we must hold that God worked his purposes out through the interaction of all these kings and their families, respecting their freedom and giving them each room for responsible decisions in much the same way as we see him doing in the rest of the histories we have just mentioned. It would not be true to the rest of the Bible were we to imagine God decreeing these events exactly beforehand and then making them happen by simply treating the humans involved as if they were marionettes, automatically controlled to produce a certain pattern of stage play. We must believe that in his providential ordering of affairs he treats the heathen under his rule as he treats his own people under his rule.

Some Old Testament scholars would hold, however, that if this

[1] *Cf.* 2 Sa. 12:11; 16:22.   [2] Gn. 45:5–8.   [3] Acts 2:23.

passage is read as a predictive prophecy, it would necessarily involve us in a view of God as working out human affairs in a purely mechanical fashion and in such a way that no decisive place at all can be given to our human choices or prayers. This consideration has driven many Old Testament specialists to deny that this is a predictive prophecy, and to insist that at least this chapter of the book must have been written up and issued at the time of the Jewish persecution under Antiochus Epiphanes. We need not take this view, however, since we believe that God can both decree and control the ordinary events of human life in the way the rest of the Bible shows him to do, and that in those days he did communicate predictively to his prophets.

Whatever view we take of the origin of the book, however, the message of the chapter stands out clearly: history as it moves towards its end can be seen to have no clear meaning. Nor will it ever be seen to have any purpose or meaning till we are able to look back on it from the standpoint of what has happened at its end and climax. The scene is dominated by men who *do according to* their *own will* (verses 16, 28), acting with reckless disregard for humanity or truth. Inter-family hatred, and especially the hatred of brother for brother, is a dominating force in development. If one finds another in the way of his overwhelming ambition, he is removed. The irrationality of the ups and downs of fortune is stressed. Some succeed, others fail badly, but there is no reason for it nor any justice in it. The hero will soon be followed by the rogue. When any noble position goes vacant there is always danger from the new occupant, and the most devastating changes can come without warning. The 'contemptible person' is always ready in the wings waiting for his opportunity which is sure to come.

It was part of Daniel's agony that he faced all this squarely. He certainly was not trying to be cynical. He described exactly what was communicated to him, as the writer of Ecclesiastes did:

> In my vain life I have seen everything; there is a righteous man who perishes in his righteousness, and there is a wicked man who prolongs his life in his evil doing. ... There is a vanity which takes place on earth, that there are righteous men to whom it happens according to the deeds of the wicked, and there are wicked men to whom it happens according to the deeds of the righteous.[1]

[1] Ec. 7:15; 8:14.

The author of Ecclesiastes, like Daniel, tries to help us to see the folly of life without God, and shows us the impossibility of making sense of things without faith in God. Daniel, possibly, takes us a step further. Where Ecclesiastes proclaimed the nonsense of life without faith, Daniel helps us to see the nonsense of trying to have faith unless at the same time we have hope in what is going to be at *the time of the end* (verse 35; *cf.* 12:4).

The transition to 'the time of the end'

We now come to a point which again tends to divide commentators very decidedly. Many believe that by the time we reach the end of this long prophecy the writer is talking clearly about what is to take place at the end of history itself. The reference in 12:4, they believe, is to this time of the end, and the whole book of Daniel closes with two further references to this final consummation of all things and all history. This view seems very justifiable, for at the beginning of chapter 12 we also have a reference to the final resurrection of the dead.

Yet there are those who believe that the book ends, and was meant to end, with the thought of the writer simply on the time of Antiochus Epiphanes. This to him *was* the time of the end. He expected all these things mentioned to happen there and then, and the book was written for the Jews who lived there and then. This view, however, is too small to fit the language of the closing section of the book, especially the opening verses of chapter 12 about the final tribulation, the resurrection, and the everlasting glory of the wise.

Where, then, does the transition from the time of Antiochus to the end of all history come? There is a view which holds that the transition to the time of the ultimate end is made somewhere in the closing verses of the eleventh, or at the beginning of the twelfth, chapter. This view implies that the description of the Antichrist figure in 11:36-39 directly describes again the pretensions of Antiochus Epiphanes (though of course it can again be taken as typical of something of later appearance and more sinister power). The following verses (40-45) are held to describe a final war in which Antiochus was actually engaged (there is no surviving historical account of such a war).

It seems preferable, however, to take the view that at verse 36 the mind of the writer is already being lifted away from the time

189

of Antiochus, *i.e.* that at this point there is at least the beginning of a switch of thought. His mind has, as we have seen, often worked with a dual reference when he thought of Antiochus, but now the further-off reference proves the stronger and his mind moves to the very end of all history. Thus, even at verse 36, the *king* referred to may be one other than Antiochus—a final Antichrist—and the descriptions of his doings, while they certainly seem to coalesce with those of Antiochus, are now meant to have a primary reference to what will take place as the whole of history is finally wound up.

This latter view helps to give point to the words of 12:4: 'But you, Daniel, shut up the words, and seal the book, until the time of the end.' The time of the end is something remote even from the historical particulars given in the detailed account of the Ptolemaic and Seleucid kings. This view of course saves us from asking which actual historical expedition of Antiochus is described in 11:40–45. Historians can tell us of nothing in the known story of this monarch which explains these verses. These would simply still remain a mystery till the time of the end really comes. In the descriptions by the later prophets of the time of the end, there is reference to a great expedition of the anti-God nations against the holy people, centred in the Holy Land and especially on Jerusalem. God finally rescues his people and annihilates their opponents.[1] Some find in this passage of Daniel a re-echoing of the same expectation of such final conflict and deliverance (*cf.* especially verse 45) which is to be re-echoed in the book of Revelation.[2]

[1]Ezk. 38, 39; Zc. 12:2–5; 14:1–5; Joel 3:9–16.
[2]*Cf.* Rev. 16:16; 19:19; 20:9.

Daniel 12
Waiting and watching for the end

The time of the end

THE beginning here is closely linked up to the end of the previous chapter and continues the great final 'vision'. By now, however, we are definitely being told about what is to take place at the end of the world. What is said here has to be supplemented and explained by what the New Testament says. At this point therefore we can try to show how Daniel points to some features in the development of history which are themselves taken up by Jesus, and re-emphasized, elaborated and thus confirmed by the writers of the New Testament. It is to this later teaching that we must turn for our understanding about the last things, rather than to the book of Daniel, though we recognize that this book helped to pioneer the way to the formation of the New Testament tradition. We have to recognize, too, that the church as a whole has never made any one particular doctrine of what is going to happen at the end into a test of orthodoxy. Those who sincerely agree on other matters may disagree about this, especially when it comes down to any matter of detail or timing. When the events of the last days really begin to take place, we will recognize them without a doubt.

The Antichrist

First of all an Antichrist has to appear.[1] The features of this ruler, who is blatantly anti-God, who magnifies himself and does according to his own will, have been drawn again for us at the end of chapter 11, with some details that are obscure and have given rise to a mass of speculation. Who is the god *beloved by women* to

[1]See pp. 144 ff.

whom this person gives no heed (11:37)? Who is the god of fortresses to whom he pays honour (11:38)? Do these references point to events in the career of Antiochus Epiphanes, or do they refer to the ruthless inhumanity of the Antichrist? Or are they simply features we have to watch for as time passes and we move towards the last days? Our Lord refers not to one great Antichrist, but to 'false Christs and false prophets' who 'will arise and show signs and wonders, to lead astray, if possible, the elect'.[1] But the apostle Paul was convinced that the end would not come till 'the man of lawlessness is revealed, the son of perdition, who opposes and exalts himself against every so-called god or object of worship, so that he takes his seat in the temple of God, proclaiming himself to be God.'[2] In the book of Revelation the figure of the final Antichrist is further elaborated. Two beasts arise which make war on the saints, achieve wonders and deceive many into service and worship. One beast bears witness to the other beast, and both bear witness to the dragon—the old serpent who has now been cast out of heaven for his last wild rampage on earth. We have thus a trinity of evil in opposition to the holy Trinity.[3]

The tribulation

The next feature of the last days, clearly emphasized, is that of *a time of trouble, such as never has been since there was a nation till that time* (verse 1). This seems to refer to trouble for the people of God, and the New English Bible is no doubt correct in its translation, *a time of distress such as has never been since they became a nation till that moment*. The church will be fearfully persecuted far more severely than Israel was under Pharaoh in Egypt, or even the Jewish nation under Antiochus. Our Lord emphasized this point very strongly in his warnings to his disciples about the days before his second coming. He seemed to refer the passage to a tribulation involving not only the elect, but also most of mankind:

> For in those days there will be such tribulation as has not been from the beginning of the creation which God created until now, and never will be. And if the Lord had not shortened the days, no human being would be saved; but for the sake of the

---

[1]Mk. 13:22. [2]2 Thes. 2:3, 4. [3]Rev. 13.

elect, whom he chose, he shortened the days.[1]

We have to remember when we face this very terrible picture that this does not necessarily mean that everything in human history favours the side of evil, even for a limited period. The tribulation is due to the tension and fear that evil has of the triumphant and developing kingdom of Christ around it. It is the increase of goodness on the earth that causes this intense reaction of evil, from the simple motive of fear. We must always remember Christ's parable of the tares and the wheat.[2] The enemy came and sowed his tares precisely where the owner of the field sowed his wheat. All attempts to uproot the tares in order to save the wheat were forbidden, and both were allowed to grow together till the harvest. It looked as if the tares had overgrown and obscured the wheat for they seemed more vigorous and natural to the soil, but when the end came, the good harvest was there unspoiled in its entirety and perfect maturity. The comment of James Denney on Paul's teaching in 2 Thessalonians is worth noting:

> The question is sometimes asked whether the world gets better or worse as it grows older, and optimists and pessimists take opposite sides upon it. Both ... are wrong. It does not get better only, nor worse only, but both. Its progress is not simply a progress in good, evil being gradually driven from the field; nor is it simply a progress in evil before which the good continually disappears: it is a progress in which good and evil alike come to maturity, bearing their ripest fruit, showing all that they can do, proving their strength to the utmost against each other; the progress is not in good itself or in evil itself but in the antagonism of the one to the other.[3]

The separation

The tribulation therefore tends to purify the genuine people of God, to confirm them in their faith, and to separate them clearly from those who are not genuine. It has the opposite effect of making those opposed to them more bold and confirmed in their godlessness. *Many shall purify themselves, and make themselves*

---

[1] Mk. 13:19, 20. [2] Mt. 13:24-30.

[3] James Denney, *1 and 2 Thessalonians* (Expositors Bible Commentary, Hodder and Stoughton, 1892), pp. 313f.

white, and be refined, but the wicked shall do wickedly; and none of the wicked shall understand; but those who are wise shall understand (verse 10). Obviously, as the end approaches, these two groups separate from each other. There is a gathering together of those who are *wise* to find fellowship under common teachers. They find help from each other and there is a purifying process till the end.[1]

The main point brought out in the book of Daniel is that none of the elect will be lost. Their names are written in the book recording God's people and God's purpose, and what is written must come to pass. But Daniel faced the problem of the multitude of individuals who had been brutally martyred in the persecution. It was not possible, knowing that God cares for justice and love, to imagine that he could be satisfied with any ultimate triumph of his kingdom that left out the multitude of the faithful people of God who had given their lives for the sake of this triumph. Daniel's faith at this point rises to the thought of a resurrection from *the dust of the earth* of those who have lost their lives in this way (verses 2f.). This implies a gathering together and a rising to life of the ashes and bones that have been scattered in the persecution, and an awakening of the souls of the dead out of their sleep. Scholars are divided as to how far Daniel's thought really goes here. The wicked are raised from the dust *to shame and everlasting contempt* as well as the elect *to everlasting life.* Some of those who limit the references in the book of Daniel to the time of Antiochus Epiphanes hold that this passage refers only to those who have been persecuted in this particular tribulation, and that the wicked referred to are the renegade Jews who committed apostasy. But this is one of the great Old Testament affirmations of the final resurrection of the body. It has a universal ring. It was when the great thinkers of the Old Testament viewed most clearly and felt most acutely the devastating effects of the power of evil, the wretchedness and injustices of the wronged and the abject misery of all innocent sufferers, that they turned their eyes upward and looked at the power, justice and love of God, and they were suddenly enabled at times to rise to their strongest and clearest expression of hope in the after life.[2] This affirmation of the resurrection arises out of this kind of experience.

[1] 11:33–35. [2] *Cf. e.g.* Is. 26:19; Ps. 73:24–26; Jb. 19:25–27.

The finale—the gap between seeing and understanding

The finale to this last great vision leaves Daniel with the sense that he has really seen to the end everything that is to be told him and unveiled to him. No more is to be added to the series of visions and auditions that have occupied his time and his mind since the first year of Belshazzar. He is now told to lay down his pen, *shut up the words, and seal the book . . . and go your way till the end* (verses 4, 13). There is complete finality in the parting gesture of the man clothed in linen who *raised his right hand and his left* (verse 7). It is like a final dismissal which lets us know that a conference is now over, and we have to go home. It must have been in Daniel's case rather like the experience the disciples had at Jesus' ascension. He had visited them time and time again during the forty days since his resurrection. He had appeared and disappeared and they had got used to expecting him to appear again. But there did come the final appearance, at the close of which 'he led them out as far as Bethany, and lifting up his hands he blessed them. While he blessed them, he parted from them'.[1] They saw him ascend, and they returned to Jerusalem with great joy, knowing that this was the decisive finale of this strange and wonderful period of learning and confirmation. Nothing more was to be added to the Gospel story and the content of the witness they were now meant to give to the world.

Daniel did not seek to delay the end of the revelation. He felt that what he had heard and seen had a fullness and authority that he could rely on, and a rich and deep meaning which, he believed, would surely unravel itself as time passed and as need arose. He had come to a basic assurance that all would ultimately be well. He knew the end would come in the time allotted by God, that evil could only play itself out, express itself only to be finally exposed and judged, and that the people of God would never be forsaken by him.

And yet he is left in deep tension. He has not understood all that he has confusedly grasped in all the visions and messages that have been brought to him. *'I heard, but I did not understand'* (verse 8). His mind has yet to grapple decisively with what has been so persistently and fully presented to him with its as yet unveiled mysteries. As this last vision comes to an end he puts two final questions to the heavenly figure who has been speaking.

[1] Lk. 24:50, 51.

195

How long will he have to wait till these things happen? And what is to be the outcome of it all (verse 6, 8)?

He receives only an enigmatic answer to the first, and none at all to the second, of these questions. It is characteristic of much of our experience of the Word of God that we have to live with this gap between our seeing and our understanding. Sometimes the Word of God, as it comes to us, brings before us realities and promises, and, indeed, visions, the truth of which we can recognize and the reality of which we can grasp by our faith, even though at the same time they are immediately beyond the scope of our understanding and reasoning processes. Sometimes, therefore, what we know we 'see' is much bigger and much more mysterious than our minds can master, or our understanding can unfold. Anyone who has begun to encounter the reality of God's presence in Jesus Christ knows that what is 'seen' here has a finality and fullness, and indeed a rationality, that is infinitely greater than the seeing and believing human mind can ever unfold. We are therefore at times in tension through having to wait so patiently and long, even in the midst of sincere and honest effort, to understand what we have seen. Yet at the same time our faith can live by, rest on, and rejoice in the truth of what it sees and hears before it understands. Daniel in his day experienced in the same way the seeing and hearing that come before understanding.

The need for steadfast patience

To grow in understanding, Daniel is warned that he will require to exercise patience and to be steadfast.

In reply to the question, How long?, he received three tantalizing answers. The first one was that the period he was inquiring about would be as long as *a time, two times, and half a time* (verse 7). The second answer was that *from the time that the continual burnt offering is taken away, and the abomination that makes desolate is set up, there shall be a thousand two hundred and ninety days* (verse 11). And then this is immediately followed with the third: *Blessed is he who waits and comes to the thousand three hundred and thirty-five days* (verse 12). Whatever this all means, it does mean, 'Blessed is he who can wait even if the dates don't work out as he expects'—even if two hundred and ninety are lengthened to three hundred and thirty-five past the thousand, and even more.

Some commentators think this gives a basis for accurate calculation even in the first answer given by this angel. They say that a *time* here means a year, and therefore *a time, two times, and half a time* means 'three and a half years'. But Calvin is much wiser:

> Its meaning is very simple [he says]. *Twice* means a long period, *times* a longer period, and *half* means the end or closing period. The sum of the whole is this: many years must elapse before God fulfils what the prophet has declared . . . as if he has said, while the sons of God are kept in suspense so long without obtaining an answer to their petitions, the time will be prolonged, nay even doubled . . . with respect to half a time, this is added for the comfort of the pious to prevent them from sinking under the delay and from despairing through excessive weariness.[1]

The main point is that before it all takes place even Daniel can come to no clear understanding of when the end is to come. Only time will reveal the times. This is why Daniel is told that his words are *shut up and sealed until the time of the end* (verse 9). We too must be prepared for the same kind of waiting, confident simply in this: that when the end comes we will know that we are experiencing what is written and that the end is upon us. Only when these things are really being re-enacted in history will we recognize them. This is why these apocalyptic passages are in the Bible—not to help us to calculate exactly, but to help us to recognize signs of the times. The prophets did not understand what exactly they were writing about. They heard and recorded their testimony about something that is much clearer to us than it was to themselves then.[2] We can, for example, understand the fifty-third chapter of Isaiah better than even its own human author centuries ago. So one day we may be able to understand this prophetic aspect of the book of Daniel better than we possibly can today.

Daniel is warned to be steadfast as he waits: '*Go your way, Daniel*' (verse 9). It means that he must continue simply as he has continued all his days. He does not need to be excited or change. He need not try to spend so much time on calculation that he has less time for his duty. The advice of the angel here is echoed by

[1]*Commentary on Daniel, ad. loc.*   [2]*Cf.* 1 Pet. 1:12.

Paul in the verses after the glorious resurrection passage in the fifteenth chapter of 1 Corinthians: 'Be steadfast, immovable, always abounding in the work of the Lord, knowing that in the Lord your labour is not in vain'[1] The way Daniel began when he risked unpopularity and yet was given favour, the way he continued when he risked everything to interpret the dream of the frantic king, trusting only in God, the way he went quietly about his routine of devotion and duty when he was basely slandered and shamefully betrayed, is the way he is to continue to the end. On this matter again we can let Paul have the last word. 'We beg you, brethren', he wrote to the Thessalonians who were tempted to lose their balance because they thought the second coming was very near, 'not to be quickly shaken in mind or excited, either by spirit or by word. . . . Let no one deceive you in any way'.[2]

The need for wisdom

As the end approaches, the times are to become hard, and courage will be needed as well as patience and steadfastness. But the times will be as tricky as they are hard, and to be courageous after choosing the wrong side and the wrong leader would end up in loss and tragedy. Therefore the stress is on the need for wisdom rather than courage. Those who contrast in the last days with the wicked are the wise: *The wicked shall do wickedly, and none of the wicked shall understand; but those who are wise shall understand* (verse 10). *Those who are wise shall shine like the brightness of the firmament* (verse 3). It is noteworthy that in many of the New Testament passages which speak of the last days, the same need for wisdom is stressed. The description in Revelation 13 of the fearful tribulations awaiting the people of God in the last days ends with the succinct remark: 'This calls for wisdom.'[3]

What is meant by wisdom is what is described in vast detail in the book of Proverbs, and as we have shown in several places Daniel himself is an embodiment of what it means to be wise. It includes an ability to discern what is phoney from what is genuine, both in people and in ways, an ability to avoid self-destructive, reckless behaviour and to choose paths that lead to life, an ability to be critical of the popular false gods who are leading many astray, and to discern just where God is speaking and what he is

[1]1 Cor. 15:58.   [2]2 Thes. 2:2, 3.   [3]Rev. 13:18.

saying. The delay in the coming of the end, and the rise of the multitudes of false Christs and false leaders as the end is delayed, will be a test of whether or not people possess such qualities. At that time the foolish, who are so easily led here and there, will become encouraged in their basic attitude of alienation from God, and bold in their folly. But at the same time the wise shine out in their wisdom, and the two types will become more and more separated. *Many shall purify themselves*, Daniel is told, *and make themselves white, and be refined; but the wicked shall do wickedly* (verse 10). This is exactly what Jesus was thinking about when he told the parable of the ten virgins.[1] Five were wise and five were foolish. While the bridegroom tarried they all slumbered and slept and no difference appeared between them. But when the final day arrived and the bridegroom came, the separation simply took place more and more as events unfolded.

The wisdom spoken about in the book of Daniel is, of course, a divine gift. While Jesus was concerned in the parable of the wise and foolish virgins primarily to stress the need for wisdom as the end approached, he also gave a hint in the story that there are dealers to whom anyone can go and buy it for themselves. He did not mean simply that there is difficulty in getting it, or that its cost is beyond anyone. He simply intended to stress again the teaching of the Old Testament, that wisdom is a gift to be sought from God and received by those who seek it, rather than a quality to be cultivated by any form of self-development or self-understanding.

The final pastoral word—the way and the place

Daniel is finally assured that he will find a path always open before him: *Go your way till the end; and you shall rest, and shall stand in your allotted place at the end of the days.* So the book ends. He is going his own way before God and is allotted a place in which he himself can stand unshaken in God's eternal presence, and find rest. In this very simple and very quiet finale, the writer is making one of the most impressive assertions in the whole Bible of the importance that God places on the individual and on his destiny in his scheme of things and in his plans for the future. He has affirmed God's control of history. He has affirmed as far as he can the resurrection of the dead. But he must bring the book to its climax by reminding those who read it that God, who calls men

[1]Mt. 25:1–13.

and women by their name, elects them to his service, and visits them in their need, also has a way for each into the future and a place for each in the new world he has prepared for those who love him. He wants us to know that in the midst of all the ravages of time, the conflicts of world empires, the strange, meaningless changes that take place in the course of world history, the man who is 'greatly beloved' cannot lose the way, and will not be allowed to be lost.

Jesus, in a like situation, knowing that his disciples were facing the same uncertainties and upheavals, assured them that if they had his presence and his fellowship they could be certain they were on 'the Way', and he said, 'I go to prepare a place for you.'[1]

The final pastoral word—the promise of rest

'*You shall rest*', said the man to Daniel (verse 13). No doubt he is to find rest while he is on the way, journeying towards the end. Obviously he already knew what this meant. In the midst of all his labour and conflict in his concern for the kingdom of God, the extreme pressures of secular business under which he must have worked most of his days, the changes of fortune that sometimes raised him up and sometimes cast him low, the slanders that must in their day have tortured him as much as they do anyone, he had had the confidence that comes from a belief in God, and the peace that comes from communion with God. In his deep concern for the future of the church and Babylon, in his agonies of prayer, and also in the long-drawn-out and deeply disturbing pastoral struggle he had to save the soul of Nebuchadnezzar, he had had at the same time a deeply assured rest of heart and mind.

The promise *You shall rest* refers also to a state that prevails in the new world to which Daniel is journeying. In the vision of that state described by John in the book of Revelation, 'the sea was no more'.[2] The sea, for the apocalyptic writers, was the home of chaos out of which the beasts arose to cause division and unrest and bitter struggle, for no other purpose than that for wickedness there can never be rest. But all this kind of conflict is over. The beasts and dragons are banished and chained where they can no longer cause hatred and stir up the restless ambitions that would dethrone God. There may be effort and toil in tasks that are challenging and ennobling for ends that glorify the Lord and his Christ, but in the midst of it all there is rest for his people.

[1] Jn. 14:2.   [2] Rev. 21:1.